D1357310

The Private Life of the Rabbit

The Private Life of the Rabbit

An account of the life history and social behaviour of the wild rabbit

R. M. LOCKLEY

INTRODUCTION BY
Richard Adams

ANDRE DEUTSCH

First published 1965 by
André Deutsch Limited 105 Great Russell Street London WC1
Second edition published 1976
Copyright © 1965 by R. M. Lockley
Introduction copyright © 1976 by Richard Adams

All rights reserved

Printed in Great Britain by
A. Wheaton & Co., Exeter

ISBN 0 233 96796 6

Introduction

To have been asked to write an introduction to this new edition of Ronald Lockley's *The Private Life of the Rabbit* gives me great pleasure, and I feel most grateful for this opportunity to express—publicly, as it were—my own deep debt to this book and to its author. Most obligations originate from personal help and mine to Ron Lockley is no exception.

When I had finished telling the story of *Watership Down* to my children (the greater part of it was extemporized to while away a long car journey from London to the Shakespeare festival at Stratford-on-Avon) and had, at their insistence, agreed to shape and write it as a novel, I realized that before that novel could hope to possess any true dignity or authenticity, then in spite of being myself a country-dweller and nature-lover, I would need to know a good deal more about the ways and lives of real rabbits. Otherwise my rabbits would be little better than cute bunnies—as too many other rabbits have become, once trapped between the ears of authors and the covers of their books. I went to a shop and looked on its shelves for a good, informative book about the English wild rabbit. Fortune was kind. What I happened upon was *The Private Life of the Rabbit*.

I quickly discovered not only how little I myself had hitherto known about "the rabbit wild and free," but also how little his true nature had been understood by the world in general. From Ron Lockley I learned that rabbits (as Strawberry protests to General Woundwort) had dignity and "animality"—the quality corresponding to "humanity" in men and women. Their life pattern was fascinating and included several phenomena not generally known. Far from being childishly cute, they possessed by nature great courage and resourcefulness within, as it were, the ambit of the limits, strength, and qualities given them by the Creator. (This I later tried to express in the story of the Blessing of El-ahrairah.) Nor were they nothing but runaways and "cow'rin', tim'rous beasties." They could and did fight their enemies—as well as each other. Incidentally, I learned, they had been anthropomorphically maligned. They were not unusually promiscuous and in many instances retained the same mate for life. (We should not, of course, think of this as particularly virtuous in an animal—that would be sentimental—but it is an interesting fact and only shows how wrong we can all persist in being about an animal once we get an idea into our heads—like the medieval notion that the pelican fed her young with blood by wounding her own breast.)

5

My hope is that *Watership Down* may play some part in leading a wider public to read Ron Lockley's book and perhaps help a little to obtain for this exceptional work of observation and natural history the wide recognition it surely deserves. For me, it is the ideal of a popular work of natural history—scholarly, concise, fascinating, and readable. We hear much today about pollution—air, water, noise, and the like—and most people have rightly become highly conscious of our danger that we may spoil the world in this way. But since we are the most powerful of the world's inhabitants and therefore the world is our responsibility (not just the world we can do what we like with), we should be equally aware of another, related danger. We need to learn more fully how to understand and respect the animals, with whom we share the world. And as civilization advances (if it does), one of our more important responsibilities must be to look after the animals. Certainly we should control them and surely we may make use of them, but we should do these things thoughtfully and we must learn not to abuse or waste the animals. Perhaps we might bear more clearly in mind (as does Milton in *Paradise Lost*) that in the creation myth of the book of Genesis, the first task given to Adam was to name all the birds and beasts. Yet it would be no good tackling our task merely by being sentimental; an animal is an animal and not a sort of human being dressed up. Before we can act wisely we must appreciate the facts and see the animals as they really are.

Ron Lockley is no sentimentalist. What he has to offer is understanding based on patient, hardheaded observation. This is why *The Private Life of the Rabbit* exemplifies what a work of natural history should be. It is the book of an excellent naturalist, of a keen, shrewd, but feeling mind and above all of a true—that is to say, a sensitive, painstaking and clear-sighted—lover of this beautiful earth (well, a lot of it is still beautiful, anyway) and of the "wondrous works of the Lord."

May 1974   Richard Adams

Contents

Illustrations

Plates 1, 3, 7 and 8 are photographs by DAVID STEPHEN

Foreword

Ah, Coney base,
Why do this harm,
With baby face
And whiskered charm!
    'The Coney in my cabbages' – E.L.G.

Why does the rabbit amuse and charm us? Most of us who are not farmers, foresters or occupiers of large gardens, smile indulgently at the sight of the rabbit in meadow, wood, or other wild environment, or in the well-fed confinement of a comfortable hutch. Perhaps the garden-poet, quoted above, may have touched on the reason?

The rabbit has a baby face, of rounded outlines, snub nose, enormous ears and eyes, and an appearance of helplessness. Konrad Lorenz has suggested that it is because of these attributes of infancy, this facial resemblance to the young human, that we – women and children especially – are pleased when we gaze at a rabbit. The fox, with its pointed nose, the badger with its pig-like profile, are less charming, even disliked and feared; we also remember the carnivorous habit of these and other long-nosed animals, and hold this, perhaps also subconsciously, against them. Yet the podgy faces of cub fox and baby badger delight us – again perhaps because of the childish appearance: rounded, helpless, without guile.

The rabbit is vegetarian, timid, retiring. It may raid the vegetable plot, but it does not attack man or man's domestic animals. Its little excursions to nibble carrots, lettuces, peas, are tiresome, but, like the misbehaviour of children whom we nevertheless love, can be corrected by our own watchfulness. Like children, the rabbits in garden, field and hutch endear themselves to us by their innocent, happy preoccupation with their simple way of living. Small wonder that in the traditional nursery tales the rabbit is both the *enfant terrible* and the lovable character. Beatrix Potter and a hundred other authors have created the acceptable image of careless, cheerful, clever Rabbit. Those enchanting Little People, the gnomes, goblins, elves and pixies, have long rabbit-like ears. Uncle Remus's Br'er Rabbit always wins in the battle of wits with Br'er Fox; Baby-face triumphs once more over Long-Nose.

Some students of human psychology have suggested that the preference for the round baby-like head, and the fear of the long, pointed mature one with thrusting nose can be traced to an old deep-seated primitive instinct in man. We accept roundness because it is a feminine shape, seductive, receptive, protective, suggestive of the welcoming shelter of the stone-age cave, the open door, the warmth of the womb and the round vaginal entrance through which the child has been expelled into this world of pain, coldness and fear, and to which it subconsciously longs to return. The long face of lean, hungry man, of savage wolf and dog, fox and ferret, is a masculine shape, destructive, often bringing terror and death, as does the pointed head of the long, forward-sliding snake; it may also have a phallic significance in the primitive subconsciousness, symbolic of the terrifying erotic power of the thrusting male organ, a seed-sower and sword ruling man's future.

It is easy to elaborate an attractive hypothesis, but perhaps better to give concrete illustrations. A pet grass-snake, perfectly harmless, evoked screams from my sisters. I had many pets as a boy, and liked snakes and rats. A white lady rat which I thought very beautiful was in appearance perhaps a compromise between female roundness and male sharpness: it had a round face and a pointed nose. But when it suddenly appeared from my sleeve women usually became hysterical. Yet their brooding maternal instinct rushed to the surface the moment that the rounded outlines of one of my young rabbits were sighted. There were oohs and ahs and a plea to be allowed to cuddle the animal.

Most of us have kept tame rabbits at some time in our lives. Next to guinea-pigs, which conveniently bring forth their young fully-furred and ready to eat grass, rabbits are one of the easiest of pets to maintain. They may be one of man's oldest domesticated animals. One can suppose that nests of wild rabbits were dug up and the young ones kept as live meat in compounds of grass at first, before man ever built hutches and cultivated crops. The origin of our domestic breeds is lost in antiquity. But we know that they are descended from the wild European rabbit, known today to science as *Oryctolagus cuniculus* (Linnaeus).

Man has, by the selection of individuals with desired characters of size, colour, structure and other heritable factors, produced an astonishing variety of 'breeds' of tame rabbits: the long-woolled Angora, the hare-like (but true rabbit) Belgian Hare, the meat and fur-bearing giants – Beveren, Flemish and New Zealand breeds, the Lop-Ear with its immense trailing ears, and many others of different colours, sizes and physical peculiarities. He has even developed a breed with fur closely resembling that of the rare Chinchilla, a small rodent found in the mountains of South America and much prized for its fur.

For some years I was to breed these Chinchilla rabbits. But as a boy I began rabbit-breeding with the handsome Old English variety; I had decided first on Belgian Hares, kept by a neighbour anxious to sell me some, but changed my mind when the buck, handled on approval, bit me severely in the arm – the Belgian Hare is notoriously quick-tempered. I formed an alliance with another boy, we built hutches out of grocery boxes, and saved up our pocket-money. When the day came to buy the nucleus, my friend, on a sudden impulse, spent most of his cash upon a toy train set. He could only afford a rather miserable thin, aged little doe. I had invested my hoarded pence in Josephine, a substantial matron guaranteed to be in 'full production'. The local rabbit-expert, known for his skill in breeding, advised us to mate our does a few days after they first came 'on heat'; by doing this, he said, we would ensure a majority of females in the litter. But if a doe was mated at the first sign of her oestrus almost all the 'kittens' would be males. He explained that this was a natural mechanism controlling wild populations: where wild rabbits were scarce and does unable to mate for several days, the delayed mating resulted in a preponderance of does which helped to build up the population rapidly; but where rabbits were numerous and does mated on the first day of heat, the potential rate of increase would decline due to the scarcity of does in the resulting litters. We believed him implicitly (but I have since found nothing in scientific literature to support this attractive hypothesis), and Josephine and the little aged doe had an interview with the buck on a day chosen in accordance with this formula which would produce a heavy majority of female kittens for our enterprise. But when in due course Josephine produced thirteen lively babies and the little doe only one tiny waif, our partnership became strained – due to dark hints from my partner's sister. It ended in a fight to vindicate my wounded pride.

This book, however, is little concerned with tame rabbits, except in this introduction to trace my own interest in this mammal, which began with keeping domestic breeds, and culminated in the study of the wild rabbit which is the subject of this monograph. I had always kept and bred tame rabbits; and years later, after leaving school and starting a small farm in a Monmouthshire valley, I dreamed of making my fortune out of breeding Chinchilla rabbits in a wild state on some small island – if I could find one. At that time all my holidays were spent in search of a suitable island, and not solely because of this money-making idea. I was a great admirer of Henry Thoreau, Daniel Defoe and others who in memorable words had described the simple life in remote and beautiful places. At twenty years of age I longed to live on a small island of my own for the sake of being close to the sea, a wide sky, wild birds, beasts and flowers.

When I found the 240-acre island of Skokholm, five miles off the entrance to Milford Haven, forsaken, surrounded by wild tides, I negotiated to take over the lease held by the last tenant, who had left the island fifteen years before. Skokholm was a marvellous place, glowing with the rose-red of its sandstone rocks, alive in summer with thousands of sea-birds, wild rabbits, and vivid maritime flowers. I sold my Monmouthshire smallholding, bought a boat and went to live on lonely windswept Skokholm. By good fortune (for me) a wooden schooner was wrecked there soon after I settled in, and with the timber and fittings from this I rebuilt the derelict farmhouse.

At that time a Chinchilla rabbit skin was worth about ten shillings. I had paid the outgoing tenant his price of £40 for the wild rabbit-crop of the coming winter, which he forecast would yield 3,000 rabbits. My simple arithmetic told me that I had only to exterminate these and replace them with Chinchillas to obtain an income of £1,500, most of it profit, since the sale of carcases would cover all overhead expenses. And £1,500 in those days was equal at least to £3,000 today.

Rabbits were introduced into Britain, it is believed, by the Normans. An interesting series of accounts is preserved in the Public Records Office showing that the Pembrokeshire islands of Skomer (Schalmey), Skokholm and Middleholm yielded what for those days were substantial profits. For example, from the Pipe Roll of Edward III we learn:

'Carcases and skins of rabbits caught in the islands of Schalmey, Schokolm

and Middleholm, Michelmas 1325 to January 30, 1326, £13 12s. Expenses:
Stipend of 3 ferreters, 12s 3d; salt for the aforesaid rabbit carcases, thread
for rabbit nets, boards, nail, and cord used for the boat in the said islands,
5s 2d.'

The present farmhouse on Skokholm may have been built around the
fourteenth-century and used by the ferreters who worked all winter for this
small wage of 12s 3d. And now I was living in it, preparing to exterminate
those rabbits brought by Norman barons. My fiancée was in charge of the
rabbitry of Chinchillas which I had started up before leaving Monmouthshire; and as soon as we were married in a year's time would bring them
with her to the island. Meanwhile I engaged rabbit-trappers who knew the
island well.

In that first winter we trapped, snared, and ferreted 2,415 rabbits, then
had to stop because the burrows were invaded in February by thousands of
shearwaters – a kind of albatross – returning from ocean to breed underground. Only two-thirds of the rabbits had been caught. In the next winter,
an all-out effort with double the number of traps caught 2,908 rabbits, again
leaving a substantial minority alive—though some of them had only three
legs left. We gave up these steel-jawed traps as thoroughly inefficient and
inhumane – they killed too many wild birds also. But snares did not work
satisfactorily, as there were few wide and flat areas where rabbits could run
fast enough to draw them. Nor were long-nets any good, for the same reason;
while ferrets, possibly because for centuries rabbits on Skokholm have known
no underground enemies such as stoats, or weasels, failed to bolt rabbits in
sufficient numbers.

On top of the failure to exterminate the wild rabbits came the depression
of the 1930s, when the market for both wild rabbit and Chinchilla rabbit
skins slumped. In the end we gave up raising Chinchillas, although for two
years we had bred them in hutches and enclosures on the island, and grown
crops to supplement their winter feeding.

In the chapter on myxomatosis I describe the first large-scale attempt in
1936 and on behalf of the Australian Government to use the virus of this
disease: this attempt was made on the isolated rabbit community on
Skokholm. Sir Charles Martin, who conducted the experiment, had asked
and obtained my permission to use it on Skokholm, having heard that I had

made previous efforts to get rid of the rabbits. Skokholm, however, proved to be an unfortunate choice of place for his research for, as the later chapter fully describes, there was a complete absence of the right vector, an absence which was peculiar to Skokholm and which nobody could have foreseen, for the vector was present on other Pembrokeshire islands. It was for this reason that myxomatosis failed at Skokholm.

In 1938 the Universities Federation for Animal Welfare offered to make the Skokholm rabbit population the subject of a demonstration of humane rabbit control, using calcium cyanide dust, which, when blown through a burrow system, produces hydrocyanic acid gas which will kill the inhabitants painlessly. A team of workers blocked the thousands of bird and rabbit holes and injected the dust throughout that winter, and reduced the rabbits from an estimated 10,000 in the autumn to a few hundred by the end of February. As a result the vegetation grew long and luxuriantly in the following summer, and we were able to graze 200 sheep and lambs.

In 1939 an attempt was made to gas out these last rabbits, most of which were now living in the cliffs and boulders close to the sea. But a world war had intervened, and the almost completely successful experiment was not carried further.

Today the rabbits are as numerous as ever on Skokholm. We had established a nature reserve and bird observatory there just before the war, which is still in full use, and many studies have been carried out since; some of those on rabbits are referred to in this book. Indirectly my experience in studying rabbit control methods at Skokholm led to an invitation from the Nature Conservancy to investigate on their behalf the progress of myxomatosis, when it broke out in England in 1953; and subsequently from 1954 to 1959 I was able to carry out a life-history study of the rabbit on my small estate of Orielton in Pembrokeshire, from which much of the information in this book is derived. For this assistance from the Conservancy, and the grant provided, I am most grateful. I would particularly acknowledge the interest and help of E. M. Nicholson, the Director-General. The Ministry of Agriculture was consistently helpful throughout this period, and I have to thank with pleasure one of their research workers, Hugh Lloyd, for reading and criticising this manuscript. My secretary at that time, F. E. Moore; Glyn Hicks; and others, also gave valuable assistance in office and field.

This book does not pretend to be an exhaustive account of the wild rabbit.

It attempts to give a picture of the social structure of rabbit communities, from first-hand observation; and I am deeply conscious of the help I have derived in making these studies from those of many other observers, a short list of which will be found on page 150 of this book.

R. M. L.

1 The Mind of a Rabbit

But learn we might, if not too proud to stoop
To quadruped instructors, many a good
And useful quality, and virtue too – WILLIAM COWPER

A warm June afternoon. From the shelter built amid the fluttering green leaves of the elm tree the observer could watch, unobserved himself, the first stirrings of the warren. It was a pleasant scene. The beautiful parkland thick with summer flowers, radiant with cowslips, comfrey, meadowsweet and bugle, wide open to the sun retreating from the zenith. Ringdoves cooed in the surrounding woods; and were answered by the cool, staccato notes of a song-thrush from the young beeches, and the liquid complaining notes of the robin.

The first rabbit to appear was a large buck with scarred ears. He emerged from the central warren, sat up, gazed round for a moment, then began to groom his coat. He licked the pads of his forepaws as he held them upturned, coating them with saliva, then pressed them down together over the sides of his face. He washed his ears by pulling each down in turn with the wet brushes of his forepaws. He washed both sides of his body with his tongue. He licked and cleaned the fur beneath his feet. This was the typical toilet of a healthy rabbit.

Suddenly he became perfectly still. He was gazing at a large hawk which had at that moment alighted silently on a fence post six feet high and thirty yards away.

The two creatures – ancient enemies, buzzard and rabbit, predator and prey – stared at each other for a long time. What went on in the mind of each? Why did both become so still? Was it due to instinct or learning (discernment), this reaction of stillness of predator watching prey, of prey watching predator? Surely there was some reasoning at work in both animals – they were not just automatons, as some observers of animal behaviour would have us believe?

An 'instinctive fear' is said to assail man when an unexpected noise, a brutal crash, or alternatively the silent surprise visit of an enemy, occurs. Our instinct is to become rigid, ready to escape, to flee, hair rising on the nape of the neck while our shocked, numbed senses presently inform us – if we are not too terrified to think – of the true nature of the disturbance, acceptable or evil.

Much the same reaction, the same instinctive fear, alarms the senses of the wild animal. All its waking hours it is subject to these alarms in its world where life is cheap and expendable, and to survive one must remain alert to each movement in the environment. But just as the human brain becomes used to and ignores the ticking of the clock, the sound and sight of traffic or of rain, the animal becomes used to and ignores those sounds and sights which do not harm it : the wind in the leaves, the songs of birds, the whirring of insects.

Probably both bird and rabbit were of the same age; the buck by the numbered tag in his ear I knew to be twenty-four months old, that is middle-aged or at least old enough to be sure of himself, and complacently able in his home environment to stare his enemy in the eye. I wondered what was going on within that tough skull, what processes of thought stirred the nerves in the grey matter of a brain which, weight for weight, was possibly twice as heavy as the brain of the hawk which glared so piercingly at the rabbit.

Both possessed large eyes, adapted to their special requirements of seeing movement over long distances, and in the dusk. In addition the rabbit had huge mobile ears which could be orientated to register and amplify all fine sounds of the moment from any direction. The buzzard was not deaf either, but its ears were small, hidden in its head feathers, and doubtless its hearing was weaker than that of the rabbit.

To understand the mind of an animal one needs at least some knowledge of the physiology of the senses of the living creature. To begin with impressions of sight, what did the buzzard see, and what was the image in the eye of the rabbit? And how near are these perceptions to those of the human observer? Not as near as Beatrix Potter's caricatures of rabbits would suggest, but perhaps nearer than the sceptics suppose.

The basic structure of the eye in bird and rabbit and human is the same : the image made by the lens falls on the nerve cells of the retina, causing a physical, chemical reaction which flashes an impulse over the nerve fibres to the brain. It is discovered that most mammals are colour blind, especially the crepuscular and nocturnal species; but birds in general have colour vision, otherwise there would be no meaning to their often brilliant plumages: and their eyes have a considerable acuity which gives them a telescopic power to see small objects clearly at a much greater distance than we can.

Probably the rabbit saw the buzzard in subdued black and white tones – and none too sharply. The bird blended into a background of trees and plants of the same black and white shades, and would be difficult to distinguish once the rabbit had looked away and lost the image, provided the bird did not move again.

The buzzard remained perfectly still on the post; the rabbit looked away, losing interest, losing the image of its enemy; and, bending down, began to graze with sweeping left and right movements of its jaws.

Very soon the buzzard turned its head to watch – with colour vision – the flight of a wood pigeon across the paddock. Experience had taught the bird that a full-grown rabbit was too powerful and difficult to tackle and kill, especially right out in the open.

As for the buck, he had not moved his head to look up at the noisy-winged pigeon, but had paused to listen, then quickly resumed his grazing. The movement of the pigeon induced reaction: on the rabbit's part a swift assessment of possible danger of attack, and on the buzzard's part an appraisal of the movement as a source of food, of killing prey, but perhaps also of possible attack by the enemies of the buzzard – man, raven, rival bird.

Without turning its head, the rabbit had directed its ears forward to catch the sounds of wing-beats, while its wide-spaced eyes, with their side and forward stereoscopic vision, saw all around in an arc of more than 180 degrees: recognising no danger in the familiar pigeon, it continued its grazing.

The buzzard, with forward directed vision, possibly of less than 180 degrees, was obliged to move its head to follow the flighting pigeon. This movement of the buzzard, though slight, was probably detected by the rabbit, which depends for survival on the ability to detect movement. But it took no further action in respect of the birds; they were not near, nor coming near enough to surprise him. He continued to feed. So the zebra of the African plains turns from the sight of its enemy, the lion, at a short but safe distance, and resumes grazing. So man reads a newspaper, beside a road along which traffic roars at fifty miles an hour. Rabbit, zebra, man are aware of safety distances and keep them.

The rabbit was living, keeping alive by two processes: eating to nourish itself, and avoiding being eaten by maintaining a safe distance from a death-dealing predator. Man is a rabbit, a zebra in habit, and consciously and subconsciously engages much of his life in the same situation, of eating to live, of avoiding death from many and numerous sources, such as war and disease, and being killed by his enemies or by the machinery which he himself has invented.

As we shall see throughout our story, humans are so rabbit.

The same organs and nerves in man, rabbit and bird achieve this self-preservation by their co-ordinated response to changes in the external scene, by interpreting and acting correctly on these external stimuli. The organs of hearing, touch, smell and taste are each connected with the seat of intelligence in the same ways as are the eyes, the organs of sight, by nerves communicating between the external sensory cells and the internal brain. External movement or stimulus causes a reaction which is automatic, and of which we and the animal are consciously aware in a greater or lesser degree. The greater the external movement the greater the stimulus and reaction upon our senses, but our reaction to these stimuli quickly becomes dulled by repetition: if we interpret the movement or sound – if it continues – as unimportant and harmless, our watchfulness declines. When the movement or sound stops it becomes a memory stored in the brain, and we almost forget it existed.

All sound is, of course, movement; and it is only movement of some kind, of light as seen by our eyes, of scent particles wafted towards our noses, or of sound-waves reaching our ears, that rouses our senses. Messages from the senses reach the brain where they are interpreted into mental images, giving 'food for thought'.

If an animal remains perfectly still, like the buzzard, making no sound, sending forth no scent, it may be completely overlooked by the newcomer, to the scene. The eye of man and rabbit, which closely resemble each other roaming over the scenery and not seeing any untoward movement, accustomed to the general overall trembling of the leaves in the summer wind, will, unless it is especially trained to pick out certain still objects, not notice the stationary figure of friend or foe against the mosaic of the background. We look at, but do not see, the speckled brown plumage of the still, silent buzzard against the multi-coloured branches and leaves, or the brown, black-stippled form of the rabbit crouched motionless in the grass. We fail to see the dappled eggs of a lark or plover in the mottled moorland at our feet and are only made aware of these as we pass them by the sudden flutter-ing escape of the agitated parent birds.

This is the so-called camouflage of nature on which so many thousands of the smaller birds, mammals and insects depend for protection against discovery by those who prey upon them.

Suddenly the buzzard glided from its post towards the buck rabbit, whose reaction was to crouch low, flattening his ears, so that he became immobile, his neutral coloured coat blending with the mosaic of flowers and grasses of the pasture. But although camouflaged to some degree by this blending of his form with his surroundings, by reduction of his stature almost to the level of the herbage, and by remaining perfectly still, he did not cease to watch the buzzard with his bold, shining eyes – which might have betrayed him. The buzzard was certainly aware of the rabbit.

The buzzard, however, was not attacking the rabbit. Its mental images were concerned, and had been concerned for some time, with other less problematic food possibilities. It pounced on something small: a vole or field-mouse, or some insect, in the grass; and flew off immediately, its scimitar talons gripping both the little victim and a few strands of vegetation.

As the buzzard glided away over the tree-tops, it uttered a long wailing cry, calling to its newly-fledged young, a signal to come to be fed. The rabbit was silent – it is silent by nature. Rabbit language is through the senses of sight, smell and hearing – the hearing of signals made by movement, of body rustling in the grass or in the burrow, or by the thudding stamp of hind feet on the ground in alarm. Vocally it has two rare sounds: a low nasal grunt, hardly audible, and used in sexual contacts; and a high treble scream or vocal squeal resembling that of a little pig, or perhaps more like that of a young child in severe distress, and it is only uttered when the rabbit is terrified, as when its life is in danger, in a trap, or when attacked by an enemy.

The buck rabbit relaxed as if a load had been lifted from his mind. He suddenly frisked, gave a little jump into the air, twisting sideways so as to come down facing half backwards. He then ran easily in a wide circle round the warren, pausing to press his chin at intervals to the ground in a forward-thrusting, almost affectionate, action. He was feeling good and playful.

Other rabbits had by now appeared, were moving about and grazing. The old buck seemed happy. He gave another little jump into the air. He ran to some dry ash from the burnt-out stump of a tree and suddenly rolled in it, like a cat in dry earth. He rose and shook himself. Then he pressed his chin against a plant stem.

The secretion of a colourless fluid from the glands beneath the jaw, which are much larger in the male, occurs when a rabbit 'chins' the ground or some plant or other object in its territory. This laying of a scent has a territorial function, advertising to other rabbits the presence of one of their kind, and in this case the territory marked and claimed.

Scent-laying or setting by a dominant male is a well-known habit in some other mammals: e.g. badger, marten, skunk, mongoose. Other animals, including the rabbit, dog and the otter, deposit faeces and urine to mark territory.

The glandular secretion is exuded from a semicircular row of pores, and becomes encrusted in a yellowish mat of fur under the chin of the young buck. The old buck's chin may become bare of fur through incessant 'chinning'. The discharge is already obvious in the buck at three months of age, but the pores are much smaller in the doe, and the fur on her chin is smooth, with only slight traces of secretion. This is doubtless in part because she is less concerned with territory-marking than her bodyguard, the mature buck. But also perhaps it is essential for her not to advertise her presence at certain times, as when she has helpless young in the nest, for the scent can also be detected by her enemies.

Our two-year-old ear-tagged buck was fully mature from eighteen months of age onwards. In about the time it takes the helpless human child to walk and utter a few simple words the rabbit has become a tough citizen of his own underworld, living in and out of burrows and able to survive and reproduce with a fecundity which is notorious. His brain at first develops more rapidly than that of the human. But the difference is rather in degree than in kind: the human brain grows more slowly, is still little developed, when the rabbit's brain is mature or is old and senile. The rabbit brain has evolved to suit its way of life, beset with many hazards, a primitive brain which translates the messages from its well-developed sense organs into what seems to us at times action of a reasoning kind, though at other times the rabbit may appear to behave in a stupid fashion.

The difference in human and animal brain power seems to lie in this far greater ability of the human to be trained and to reason from training and experience, to use tools thoughtfully, to be aware and react intelligently and enterprisingly to changes in the environment. If the rabbit were as long lived as man, tortoise, elephant, whale or dolphin (to name a few long-lived and intelligent animals) perhaps it too would improve its intellectual stature over the years.

Such speculation is vain and unprofitable. We know much about the anatomy but little about the mind of the animal. As to intelligence, all we really know is that the domestic rabbit, studied in hutches, has a capacity for learning slightly inferior to that of a domestic cat. Both animals when young can be trained to perform simple tricks, play games and be affectionate. But they die too soon for us. They are middle-aged at five and senile at ten years of age.

We know so much less about the wild rabbit which even when taken very young from the nest in the field and hand-reared does not easily, if indeed ever, become tame. The process of breeding up the present domestic varieties from the original wild source has occupied many centuries of handling in captivity, selective breeding and the exploitation of mutations, or 'sports'.

The field naturalist finds it extremely difficult to study in a completely wild state an animal which lives underground for most of the day, which comes forth to feed above ground largely by night, and which hides its newborn young deep in the earth. Its habit of running to cover when it sees man, and indeed living much in the cover of woodland, copse and hedge make it correspondingly difficult to study as an individual. But until we are able to study the individual we cannot begin to know the truth about its life-history.

For this reason we found it necessary, when we began a full study of the life history of the rabbit, to adopt certain measures to establish a colony of rabbits under some degree of control.

It was a time when the fatal disease of myxomatosis had ravaged rabbit populations in France and had arrived, in late 1953, in Kent. If the disease should spread over the British Isles and have the same effect as it had had in

France, then the resulting disappearance of the rabbit would have far-reaching effects on agriculture, forestry, gamekeeping, and nature generally. The swards of rabbit-bitten farmland, downland, sand dunes and wild wastes, many now being, or soon to be, declared as nature reserves, would change considerably. Without rabbit-grazing, the character of commons, downs, warrens, covert and woodland might alter out of all recognition.

This impending change was of special concern to the naturalists and conservationists; in particular the Nature Conservancy of England, Wales and Scotland would need to study the effects on their wildlife reserves.

It was discovered, almost in a panic, that little was known, first about myxomatosis in Britain, and secondly, about the life of the rabbit. There was a public demand for more information and a special Myxomatosis Advisory Committee was set up by the Government. The Nature Conservancy invited me to conduct research into both these subjects. The results are described in the succeeding chapters.

2 The Coney Garth

Master Rabbit I saw
In the shadow-rimmed mouth
Of his sunny cavern
Looking out to the South — WALTER DE LA MARE

The present Orielton estate is the relic of a much larger property of nearly 12,000 acres. The manor house stands in a wooded demesne of 260 acres surrounded by high walls, a little isolated forest in the windswept treeless south-western peninsula of Pembrokeshire, itself the south-westernmost county of Wales. The name is probably Norman, perhaps given to it by the first Norman owners, the eleventh-century knight Wirriet or Wyriot into whose hands it was delivered as a reward for services in William the Conqueror's army of invaders.

The first reference to the Wirriet family appears to be by Geraldus Cambrensis (Gerald the Welshman), the twelfth-century historian and prelate who lived a few miles away at Manorbier Castle, where no doubt like other feudal lords he kept a rabbit warren. Rabbits were at that time new to Britain, introduced it is generally believed by the Norman conquerors, part of whose equipage was a warrener and his ferrets. (Gerald, who travelled in Ireland, is the first writer to note the presence of rabbit warrens in that island.)

The Wirriets and their descendants held Orielton for 700 years, to the middle of the nineteenth century. They were gentlemen, at times knighted, born to privilege, men of fame or notoriety: they supplied members of of parliament, sheriffs, and honorary officers of this and that. They had from the beginning established an efficient feudal system, with columbarium, fish-ponds, rabbit-warren, mill and private army.

The fish-ponds and columbarium remain, the mill decays, the private army is now a shifting crowd of young naturalists which inhabit, week by week, the lovely old house – for it serves today the excellent purposes of a field study centre.

To this day one of the principal fields near the old house is locally known as 'Coneygar', that is, the Coney Garth, Norman term for a rabbit enclosure or warren. This field, surrounded by a shelter belt of trees, is typical of a twelfth-century Norman warren.

We did not use the Coney Garth as such. For convenience, we established our warren in the parkland in front of the manor house where on wet days we could watch rabbits even from the big windows. Here one looked eastwards over a tree-embowered lawn of four acres which sloped gently to a broad pond where a pair of swans lived. Yellow flags, mimulus and purple loosestrife fringed the banks, and water lilies whitened the surface, in spring and summer; in the evening little fishes splashed the mirror reflecting the magenta of rhododendron and camellia blossom, and the stare of statuesque herons.

In the centre of the East Lawn stood a decaying elm, centuries old. Long ago it had lost its great crown, possibly struck by lightning. But as is the way of elm, from its sapwood stump, broken off at twenty feet high, it had sent skywards a palisade of straight and youthful boughs. This made a perfect bower or hide into which, after a rustic ladder and a little roof of green-painted material had been added, one could climb and observe the warren in comfort in any weather, unobserved by the inmates.

Around this elm in open grassland we established the enclosure by erecting a six feet high wire-netting fence, sunk into the ground, rabbit proof and fox proof, and dividing it into pens, as described below.

The climate of Orielton is mild and humid, suited to the Mediterranean origin of the rabbit, which does not thrive in prolonged cold, severe frost and snow. Frost is comparatively rare at Orielton, perhaps on a dozen nights in a normal winter thin ice may form on the Lily Pond. Snow never lies long; in some winters none falls. The annual rainfall is low, for Wales; averaging about thirty-six inches. Summer day shade temperatures rarely exceed twenty-one degrees centigrade; the range of temperature is small, due to the stabilising effect of the Gulf Stream or west wind drift from the Atlantic, whose waters invest the peninsula on the north, west and south sides.

The parkland of the East Lawn has rarely or never been ploughed since it was first drained and levelled from forest, probably in the days of the first Norman settlers. It has been grazed or mown for hay each summer. When in the summer of 1954 I bought the estate (the manor and 260 acres within the walls) the East Lawn was a rabbit-bitten mosaic of wild flowers, beautiful to the naturalist but considered as grossly deteriorated pasture by the farmer. I was both naturalist and farmer, by profession and inclination.

Cowslip and primrose, celandines and other buttercups in number, bugle and bluebell, ground ivy and little and big sorrels, dock and comfrey, wood-rush and plantain, self-heal and daisy and dandelion, lords-and-ladies, twayblade, birdsfoot and hop trefoils, wild clover and other trefoliums, wild raspberry, strawberry and blackberry, violet and veronica, thistles and nettles; and over all the rose-and-yellow-white sheen of meadowsweet and honeysuckle. These made up the vivid pattern and sweet scent of the parkland viewed from the east front of the manor, satisfying to the naturalist and the idle viewer. Nor were all the grasses between the flowers such as to please the farmer: plenty of Yorkshire fog, meadow grass, foxtail, dogstail, sweet vernal grass, fescue, and some cocksfoot. Elm suckers and rhododendron were encroaching from the north side woods.

A full plant list was compiled and regular transects over four years were subsequently to reveal the changes due to different pressures of rabbit grazing.

There was no natural water in these enclosures. At first we supplied shallow pans of fresh water, but the rabbits were never observed to drink.

Plate 4 shows the general layout of the enclosures. As we wanted to test the adaptability and capacity of the rabbit in relation to a common standard area of ground, we divided the twelve acres of enclosed land into five areas (Fig 1):

Intensive Pen A/B One acre.

Two half-acres, connected by controlled passageways, for the study of a maximum number of rabbits, building up from a strong nucleus of six pairs.

To avoid the use of symbols we called the half-acre A 'Plain'; and the half-acre B, 'Wood'.

Extensive Pen C One acre, known as 'Savanna'.

This enclosure was designed for the study of a very small colony of rabbits with an extensive grazing range, for which purpose the breeding population

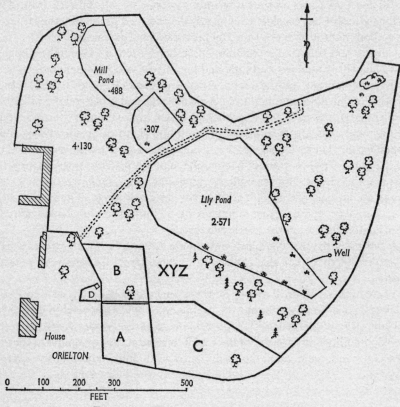

FIGURE I. The study enclosure at Orielton

was limited to one buck and two does, their progeny being removed at weaning age (one month) or as soon as they might be caught before they were old enough to have much effect on the grazing.

This pen 'Savanna' was equivalent to a local farm field, where normally rabbits in small numbers grazed pasture, which (on the farm) was either cut for hay or grazed by farm stock. As three adult rabbits could not keep down the grass on one acre, this pen was periodically grazed by sheep, with the effect that the grass was reduced to a height suitable for the observation of the rabbits therein.

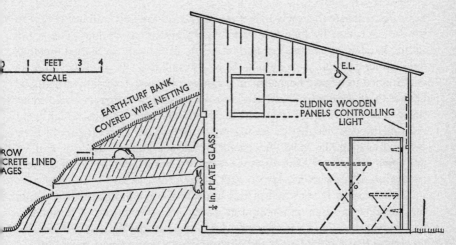

FIGURE 2. Diagram (elevation) of artificial warren for observing rabbits underground

Artificial Warren D (Fig 2) 'The Underground'.

This was designed for the purpose of studying the behaviour of the rabbit below ground. An artificial warren system was built of concrete, mounded with earth, with a vertical face of plate glass eight feet wide and four feet high, displaying the concrete-lined burrow in section (see Plate 5). The approach to the interior living quarters for the rabbits was by way of concrete tunnels four to six feet long, sufficiently constricted to permit the passage of an adult, but not wide enough for one to rest comfortably in; in practice the occupants of the artificial warren preferred the roomy burrows opening against the glass, and did not linger in the entrances and exits except occasionally when frightened by the activity of the human observer beyond the plate glass. The earth bank covering the concrete tunnels was secured from burrowing by wire netting pegged to the earth.

The observer was comfortably housed in the weatherproof hut which protected the glass from outside interference. This hut was timber built, roofed with corrugated iron, and lit by mains electricity. The floor space was eight feet by eight feet; the sloping roof six feet high. There was room for a screen, a chair and a table. Access to the hut was by a low door on the north side. The whole of the lower half of the interior of the west wall was occupied by the eight feet by four feet plate-glass observation window. Two small sliding hatches, one in the east and one in the south wall, were used to admit daylight to the hut as required. It was found that the rabbits could be conditioned to behave normally underground in both daylight and artificial light if these were introduced gradually. Also that the observer could move slowly and quietly near the glass without disturbing the rabbits, which spent most of the day sleeping or resting in the burrow, often with part of their bodies touching the glass. A curtain from roof to floor made a kind of anteroom around the little entrance door, screening the light therefrom and concealing the observer's arrival and departure.

The enclosure D consisted of this hut and the mound of earth covering the concrete entrance passages, and giving access to a plot of permanent pasture enclosed in a rabbit-proof wire-netting fence. By trial and error it was found that a plot of grassland of approximately 250 square yards sufficed to feed two adult rabbits throughout the year (equal to just under forty rabbits per acre). It provided barely adequate grazing in dry years, and more than enough grass in a wet summer.

Apart from its importance in studying the rabbit below ground, enclosure D enabled us to evaluate the appetite and behaviour of the individual rabbit.

The 'wild' enclosure XYZ

This was intended as a natural control with a small population of wild rabbits contained within approximately twelve acres of woodland, marsh, water and grassland (Fig 1).

Two young does and a buck of the year were ferreted from near-by farms and turned down in November 1955. This nucleus disappeared in the cover of the woodland east of the Lily Pond and the trio were seldom seen. They or their descendants were present throughout the three succeeding years as a small colony; but they were much shyer than the enclosed rabbits from Skokholm. It would have been difficult to follow their affairs closely in the shelter of the trees and scrub, and impossible in the limited time. Watching from the tree hide, we occasionally saw one emerge from cover and approach the wire fence enclosing B or C. At night their pellets were dropped along the boundary fence. Two nests were dug out in the woods, and found to contain three and five young respectively; no significance was attached to these isolated records however. This wild colony illustrated the impossibility of adequately observing rabbit populations in coverts and wooded environment, a common habitat.

Establishing the nucleus

By the time the pens were ready the virus of myxomatosis was rampant in Britain. It had spread both naturally and artificially (by man) since the initial appearance in the south-east in the winter of 1953–54; it had reached the abundant rabbit colonies of Pembrokeshire by the autumn of 1954. The woods and fields of Orielton swarmed with rabbits which were damaging both the young trees and the pasture.

Myxomatosis travels fastest, like all fast-working lethal viruses, through a dense population; this is because the close proximity between individuals of a crowded colony ensures a rapid continuous chain of infection. It reached Orielton late in 1954; within a couple of months it destroyed approximately 199 out of every 200 rabbits, that is, it virtually exterminated the rabbit population; leaving behind one or two scattered immune individuals.

We were suddenly faced with the problem of studying an animal which had disappeared from Orielton! Even the odd immunes, if such they were, had fled from the few burrows on the East Lawn and were seen no more. Our enclosures of rabbit-proofed netting, six feet high, and sunk deep in the ground, were ready to be operated, but we could not find any live rabbits to lay down a nucleus.

The Ministry of Agriculture detailed the local Pests Officer to help us find some wild rabbits. We went to warrens by the sea in Pembrokeshire where rabbits were still reported to exist. With ferrets to drive them from burrows, we netted seventeen and placed them in quarantine in hutches.

Myxomatosis will kill its victim in about ten days from the moment that an infected flea from a myxomatous rabbit bites a healthy rabbit (the virus is carried as a contaminant on the sucking mouth-parts of the flea). These rabbits were vaccinated with an anti-myxomatosis serum, known as the Fibroma of Shope, which had been used to protect domestic rabbits and was considered to convey immunity against the disease for a period of about nine months in ninety per cent of vaccinates.

Of the seventeen rabbits thus collected locally thirteen died of myxomatosis in spite of positive injections of the fibroma serum; evidently some were already infected at the time of capture. Only one doe and two bucks were left sufficiently healthy and vigorous to put down as breeding stock. It was a poor beginning. A few more does at least were essential. What would happen if we let this triangle of two males and one female loose in the enclosures? Would the males fight or would both harry the female too much?

But we must not keep them in hutches longer than a few days, which was long enough to determine whether they would or would not develop the lethal disease of myxomatosis. The wild rabbit fretted and often would not eat food in the confinement of a rabbit hutch; it lost condition rapidly. We marked and released the trio in the Intensive Pen (half-acre A) Plain.

FIGURE 3. Chick wing-tag for ear-marking rabbits
a – open   *b* – closed

Chick wing-tags (Fig 3) were used for marking individuals, and proved so completely successful that other methods were not tried. These tags are fastened by a curved pin which is clinched over flanges at each end of the flat aluminium plate approximately ¼ inch square. A recognition number was painted on each side in black enamel over a white enamel base, the numbered tab was pinned low over the strong dorsal ridge of the ear close to the nape, and could be fitted painlessly through the thin membrane and clinched with pliers. In this position it was conspicuous and easily read both frontally and from behind. Also it did not easily tear out in this position around a strong ridge of gristle. At the same time the same number was tattooed higher up in the thin semi-transparent membraneous part of the ear with a small tattooing pliers and indelible black ink; these tattooed numbers were effective and most of them remained legible throughout the experiment as a check in case the tag was lost. In a good back light the tattoo could sometimes be read through a telescope from the hide at a distance of up to 100 feet.

Males were tagged and tattooed in the right and females in the left ear; thus the sexes could be recognised in the field even if the figure on the tag was obscured by dirt or distance or by the inconvenient position of the marked rabbit in relation to the observer.

Sex, weight and age were recorded for each newly marked individual together with degree of infestation by parasites (chiefly rabbit fleas) and other notes, such as variation of coat colour and the size and shape of the occasional white mark on the forehead. The age of the young rabbits born each season in the enclosures could be estimated fairly accurately to the nearest month; and if necessary we could apply a simple test – although in practice it was not always reliable. In the rabbit the ossification of the growing part of certain bones, of the apophysis with the diaphysis bones of the tibia, does not take place until it is about ten months old; if the soft cartilagenous gap between these bones can be felt with the thumbnail the animal can be estimated to be less than ten months' old.

Recaught rabbits were weighed again, and examined in the same way. A card index was used to record the data of each individual, and a loose-leaf field diary was used to record their movements observed at the watchpost in the elm tree and in the hut which housed the underground observation window.

The three surviving rabbits were dusted with flea powder and placed in Plain (the intensive Pen A) where they enjoyed the dry shelter of a large wooden box, mounded with earth and with a tunnel access to the grazing. In new surroundings they would need some comfort, a warm, dry roof – for it was now February, cold and wet. They had the freedom of half an acre of grassland.

In spite of dusting with insecticide all three immunised rabbits when examined a month later were carrying fleas on ears and head; those must have come from the burrows in or near which fleas had survived (as adult or larvae) after the last rabbits had died of myxomatosis, and the hungry fleas had hopped on to the new arrivals.

A rare snow fell at intervals during February. The three rabbits scratched the snow from around the beaten tufts of withered grass surviving from summer's surplus and pulled the long tough dried stalks out, chewing the juicy base, and scattering the rest.

Seven, the larger male, ear-tagged and tattooed with the number 7, had assumed possession of the one female (whom we dubbed 'Mrs Potter', but her ear-tag was 4). He allowed the other buck, Three, no nearer approach to Doe Four than half a dozen lengths, say six feet. As soon as this distance was reduced Buck Seven darted towards Buck Three, who timidly retired.

This was the first indication of what is a common phenomenon in animals, even in man: territorial behaviour. The territory was defended by the dominant male and appeared to be movable, a charmed circle with the doe at the centre. But as yet, in the cold early spring of 1955, the three rabbits did not show themselves much during the brief hours of daylight; all we could discover in one or two observations of a fine afternoon was that Buck Three was having the worst of it, was unwelcomed or at least ignored by Mrs Potter, and ill-treated by the powerful Buck Seven.

Where could we obtain more rabbits for our enclosures?

The only flourishing colonies of rabbits surviving after the myxomatosis epidemic were those living on certain isolated islands. It was discovered that Skokholm, some seventeen miles as the crow flies from Orielton, remained free of disease during the severe myxomatosis epidemic of 1953–55. So it was to Skokholm that we had to go to obtain enough live rabbits to ensure the nucleus for our observation enclosures.

In March 1955 we obtained by ferreting at Skokholm two bucks and three does; and in June 1955 a further consignment of two adult bucks and two adult does (together with two young bucks and four young does born in that spring). The first batch were introduced in Plain (Pen A) on March 15th; the second into Wood (Pen B) on June 22nd.

From the life histories of these rabbits and their progeny is drawn the material on behaviour in the succeeding chapters.

3 The Nucleus

The litel conyes to her play gunne hye – CHAUCER

In a monograph on another burrow-nesting animal, the Manx shearwater, on Skokholm, we described how we marked each bird with a serially numbered leg-ring, by which it could be identified as an individual, and its movements and habits recorded. Later, as we became more intimate with the characters of this study, we began to give the birds names, beginning with A for the first pair (Adam & Ada), B for the next pair (Bill & Bess), C for the third pair (Carol & Caroline), etc.

In our study of individual rabbits at Orielton it was some months before certain leading rabbits became familiar to us by their frequently observed behaviour and characteristic habits. But as soon as they exhibited these idiosyncrasies regularly we began to apply names – at first without a plan, and most of them uncomplimentary. Thus Buck Seven became known as 'Rough Stuff', Buck Three was nicknamed 'Weary Willie', Buck Twenty became 'Timid Timothy' (this name was to stick), while the powerful Doe Four was dubbed 'Mrs Potter' (afterwards changed to 'Beatrix').

Then, as information began to pile up in the daily log, we adopted a systematic arrangement of names related to the ages of the rabbits. Names beginning with A were to signify rabbits born in 1953 or earlier, with B those born in 1954, C in 1955, D in 1956, and so on.

In practice when making accurate notes in the field it was necessary for clarity, as well as simpler, to jot down the ear-tag of the rabbit under observation, as seen through the binoculars or telescope. It was only when writing this book that we have exchanged that number for the name given to the rabbit and written under its number on its index-card in our files. We have used the names here because we believe that to do so instead of numbers is less confusing to the reader, and may even impart something of that delightful feeling of intimacy with these characters which we enjoyed in the many hours of watching a wild animal endowed with much charm and not a few of those emotions and actions common to man himself.

The three mainland born rabbits had settled down in Plain as already related and were socially adjusted to the situation of the large adult buck Big Boss (7) living with Beatrix (4), while the smaller buck Born Tired (3), probably less than a year old, was permitted only to graze and live at a distance. Big Boss, healthy and plump, reigned supreme over the abundant, rough pasture of the enclosure. Born Tired was in very poor condition. He seemed to have little will to live; but he courted their company. Evidently he did not like to be alone – this study was to confirm that the rabbit is essentially a gregarious animal. Born Tired would sneak into the shelter of the elm logs, under the cover of the green corrugated iron canopy we had provided, and in which the paired couple Big Boss and Beatrix were happily 'married' and breeding in the spring of 1955.

It was therefore a rude interruption to the settled state of this pair when on March 16th two adult bucks and three adult does caught at Skokholm were introduced into the same half-acre enclosure Plain.

It was getting lighter each evening; the rabbits came out to catch the late sun. It was pleasant to sit in the Tree Hide and watch the events below. Even if the rabbits were slow to emerge after the disturbance of the observer's arrival, climbing of the ladder, and positioning himself in the elm look-out, there were always birds to watch and listen to, on the lily pond, in the

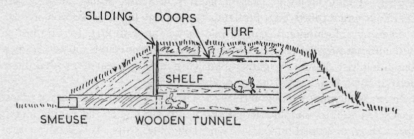

FIGURE 4. The box-warren, A.S.W. (central section)

meadows, in the trees. A flock of one hundred crows would regularly arrive before dusk and with raucous conversation drift across the sky to settle to roost in the distant treetops.

The five island-born newcomers had been popped into holes (Fig 4) at ASW (= Pen A, South-West warren), leaving ANE (= Pen A, North-East warren) to the three mainlanders.

These Skokholm rabbits, accustomed to graze early in the day, since there are no ground-living mammals save man, no foxes, badgers or dogs, to disturb them on that island, came out of their new homes earlier than the mainland rabbits did. It was interesting to find that the dominant mainland Big Boss immediately adapted his activities to those of the islanders. This was evidently because he was stimulated by the newcomers and found it necessary to attempt to dominate them and keep his position as king-buck of Plain.

Big Boss proceeded to patrol the whole of Plain with much more attention than when he had only Born Tired to dominate. He now had to acquaint two other bucks (20 and 21) with his authority; as well as advertise his maleness to the new females (18, 19 and 22).

The behaviour of the four males and four females in dawn and late afternoon watches was recorded in diary form, as it happened (to the nearest minute of each hour).

Big Boss paraded the enclosure, hopping towards each rabbit near him which he could smell or see. If the rabbit was still and crouched down he might overlook it, or locate it by catching its scent, as he extended his head and neck, 'winking' his sensitive nostrils, twitching them to reveal the curious sensory pads which probably receive the distinct sex scent of each individual rabbit, male and female, and convey that distinction to the brain. If the female was in a receptive or oestrous condition the buck would receive the olfactory signal more clearly and act accordingly; only thus can one account for the readiness with which a buck ran up to and courted some females, while ignoring others.

But most rabbits were detected by direct sighting as they made grazing and other movements.

Big Boss required each of these rabbits to move out of his way when he approached to investigate. If it did not, he would take one of five courses of action:

(1) attack by running towards it rapidly. This was the most frequent course of action.

(2) graze slowly towards it, nibbling the grass in quick desultory mouthfuls; this was evidently both a 'displacement' activity (releasing some of the energy building up for an attack) and a form of threat; it would end in Big Boss attacking if the rabbit did not retreat.

(3) hop with a curious stiff-legged gait, the white scut well up on rump, and hind feet almost on tip-toe and not flat to ground as in normal walk, moving usually in a diminishing half-circle around the rabbit concerned; a movement which showed the broadside and white belly and scut of the back to greater advantage, so that he appeared larger and more formidable (Fig 5). This was a form of intimidation, like the display of a cat with its hair

FIGURE 5. Rabbit in hostile attitude

on end or of a dog walking stiff-legged and bristling around another before a fight. In this semi-circular parade the buck might rub his chin on the ground or some small object in his path, smearing droplets of male scent and in effect marking the ground as his territory. If the object of this display did not retreat the buck would attack.

(4) scratch at the ground with forepaws. Another dog-like activity and a displacement-display of energy preliminary to an attack. It might be accompanied by a depositing of faecal pellets upon the displaced earth or grass.

(5) squirt urine, often apparently aimed at the other rabbit, by a sudden leap and sideways flick of the elevated hindquarters during the stiff-legged

parade. This was the least frequent course of action. To the human nose the smell of the buck's urine is strong and its release must advertise the visit of a mature buck to another rabbit in no uncertain fashion.

Big Boss behaved in a manner typical of any dominant buck observed in the enclosures in the next four years. He was most aggressive towards other bucks, but often showed no desire to intimidate does. He would sniff the air as if to inform himself of the sexual condition of a doe, then pass her by. Unless she was actually in his line of patrol he rarely troubled her. If she found herself in his path, she would usually take avoiding action and run out of his way. She recognised and feared him. He might, but usually did not, chase her in what was a sexual rather than a territorial pursuit, or a mixture of both.

To his mate Big Boss behaved differently. He behaved like a loyal, courteous husband, even as if he were a little afraid of offending her. Indeed, if she was not in a mood to accept his amatory attention, she might even snap at him, by striking towards him with her forepaws. Or she would dodge him impatiently. These were signals to leave her alone; and he obeyed. She gave such signals when she was hungry and grazing; or when occupied in making a nest.

At other times, when the sun was shining perhaps, and she had grazed enough, she would relax, often lying down on her side, exposing the white fur of her full belly. She then permitted him to sit beside her, and lick her fur. He appeared to enjoy licking her forehead, ears and neck. Sometimes, though not often, she would lick his face. After such a preening session the couple might remain together, side by side, or facing each other, calm, relaxed, idle.

Sometimes they played together, when she was in a mood for it. There would be a time of attractiveness lasting several nights when the buck chased the doe in little circles, or he was chased by her, a kind of nuptial dance. She did not, however, submit to the mating until the last night of attractiveness, the hour of strongest libido. During the breeding season the adult female wild rabbit becomes sexually attractive to the male, it is believed, at approximately seven-day intervals. At about the seventh day, there is a period of heightened attractiveness when she is not only ready to mate but will seek out and court the male.

As we shall see, the sexual life of the doe is related to the number seven. Her period of gestation is about $7 \times 4 = 28$ days. She will litter each month during the breeding season at about thirty-day intervals. And it is believed that she mates usually about every seventh day during the eight months or so that the buck is fertile and potent.

In her relations with other females we were to find that the doe was not unduly aggressive. Provided another, secondary, female did not cross her path, the dominant doe rarely attacked, especially in the early uncrowded days. There were frequent slight displays of thrusting head or forepaws towards a visiting doe by the resident doe, and usually the visiting doe at once moved off. Invasion of her nesting burrows, however, by an alien doe, would lead to a chase until the intruder was expelled.

Big Boss succeeded in dominating the newly arrived bucks 20 and 21 (Timid Timothy and Bold Benjamin). Poor feeble Born Tired continued to decline; he failed to secure a mate. Even though there was a spare female available he failed to court her. Big Boss secured her.

On April 9th all eight rabbits were caught in the artificial burrows (Fig 4) for a check-up of condition. Born Tired was very thin and his testes quite small and soft. He seemed likely to die, and as we feared he might have an infection which could pass to the seven other healthy inmates, he was removed and put out of his misery.

In the field, the simplest assessment of fertility in the buck is by the size of the testes. The testes of male rabbits become enlarged and fill the scrotal purse at the commencement of the breeding season, and can be seen as two pinkish kidney-shaped organs covered with semi-transparent brown skin between the hind legs. After the breeding season they regress and become flaccid, and are withdrawn gradually into the abdomen over the resting period in early autumn.

On April 9th the testes of Big Boss were fully projected, heavy and hard, more so than the well-developed testes of Timid Timothy and Bold Benjamin. All three were in full breeding condition. Big Boss and Bold Benjamin were probably the same age, born early in 1954. But Timothy appeared older and although lighter in weight than his co-islander Benjamin, he was scarred and worn-looking, as if he had had many and not always successful fights in the past. Probably he was born in 1953 or earlier.

Mainland-born Big Boss was half a kilogram heavier on the scales than the Skokholm bucks. His weight was added to the advantage of being in possession of the best territory in Plain. But he did not achieve dominance unchallenged by the vigorous Skokholm born Benjamin. They were seen to fight on three occasions by day, and doubtless many scraps passed unobserved in the darkness of night.

Bold Benjamin was a strong character and he secured as a mate Bertha (18) and dwelled with her under the meadowsweet covering the warren ASW farthest from his enemy Big Boss.

As for Timid Timothy, he was observed to frequent the corridor of grassland (Fig 6) between the main warren ANE (=Pen A, North-East

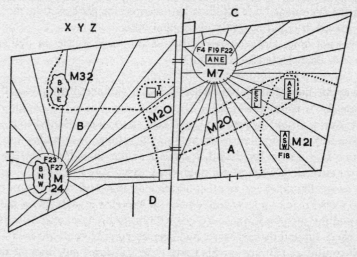

FIGURE 6. Territories of bucks in A and B, June 1955. Circles with radiating lines – warrens and range of dominant bucks; pecked lines – limits of range of each secondary buck. The does were sedentary, grazing near home. M – male. F – female.

warren) where Big Boss lived with his first wife Beatrix and two other does (we might perhaps call these concubines), Bianca and Blanche, and the little warren ASW, where the other mated pair lived. But he had no mate that we could properly claim was his. He was an outcast, frequenting empty burrows and often lying out on fine nights in a far corner, alone. He was never a success, though he was to live long.

Although Beatrix had all the advantage of being first lady or queen to king Big Boss, she was not obviously pregnant when handled on April 9th. But then she was a young doe, probably under a year old; nevertheless because of her size (a mainland size) heavier than the older Skokholm does, she looked adult. Possibly she had come into breeding condition later on account of her tender age; or she may have mated and conceived, but failed to produce live young – a not uncommon phenomenon in the wild rabbit.

Two of the Skokholm does, Bianca and Blanche, were pregnant on April 9th; but Bertha was not. Thus the first litters in the enclosure were born, in April, not to the leading lady Beatrix, but to the concubines from Skokholm which the dominant buck Big Boss had secured for his harem in the commodious and dry quarters under the roof of ANE.

It was not long, however, before Bertha produced a litter of five in her home with Bold Benjamin at ASW.

This was the 'state of the parties' when the other half-acre Pen B, 'Wood', was colonised by a consignment from Skokholm consisting of two adult bucks Bright Star (24) and Brown Boy (32), two adult does, Beautiful (23) and Bronwen (27), together with six half-grown rabbits (two males and four females). This was on June 22nd, 1955, a date late enough in the season to expect no further breeding from does which must have been psychologically upset by the handling and resettlement in a strange and alien environment.

The finest, driest and deepest warren in Wood was at BNW, a bank of earth and the site of a strong colony of wild rabbits before myxomatosis had killed them out and the enclosures had been erected. Here Bright Star settled with Beautiful and Bronwen; his testes were still firm, but those of Brown Boy were softer, beginning to regress and he did not secure a mate. He settled alone in BNE, a rather damp natural burrow system, and was confined in his grazing to the SE quarter of Wood; Bright Star did not at first permit him to visit BNW except by stealth.

Figure 7 illustrates a sample plan we made of the approximate patrolling movements of the dominant bucks in Plain and Wood at this time.

It was near the end of the normal breeding season, however, which terminates in Wales with a few last litters born in July. Territoriality was beginning to slack off as male fertility declined.

For the first time we opened the two underground tunnels linking the half-acres Plain and Wood (Fig 8).

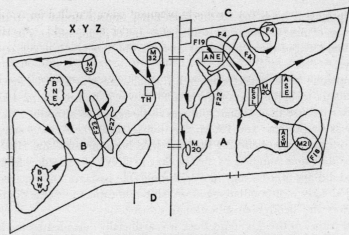

FIGURE 7. Approximate patrolling movements of dominant bucks and their encounters with does and secondary bucks: buck M 24 (Bright Star) in B, 1600–1900 GMT, June 29th, 1955; buck M 7 (Big Boss) in A, 1600–1900 GMT, June 25th, 1955.

The outcast Timid Timothy immediately passed through, to try his luck in Wood, having been so ill-treated in Plain. But he met opposition from Bright Star and Brown Boy. They drove him back. He was between two fires.

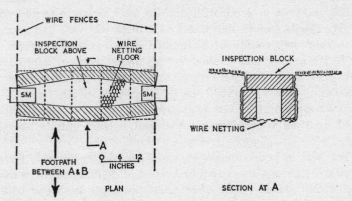

FIGURE 8. The underground passage between A and B in plan and cross-section. SM, smeuse or catching box.

He compromised by living in the connecting tunnels under the concrete blocks, now coming forth to graze along the edge of Plain, and now in Wood. Timid Timothy hid there, an ageing unsuccessful 'bachelor', in this neutral territory.

The opening of the passages between the half-acres was now the signal for a general mix-up of the two populations. Plain was on higher ground and also had better pasture than Wood, and was in theory more attractive. But the new bucks Bright Star and Brown Boy remained at their new warrens in Wood; as did the dominant Big Boss and Bold Benjamin in Plain. However, the two adult does adopted by Bright Star in BNW were restless from the start and did not breed – they moved through the passages and entered the dry and already well-populated warren ANE and came under the dominion of Big Boss and Beatrix, as subordinate subjects.

The territory of the dominant Buck was artificially curtailed by the limits of the enclosures. We wondered how much territory a dominant buck could control. The opening of the tunnels connecting Plain and Wood took place at a moment when there was a truce to sex and its jealousies, when there was little or no fighting, and no mating because the bucks were physically with regressed testes and showed no libido.

In October the moult was complete. The truce was over. The bucks began to reassert themselves, and the sorting out of territories among the old and the young breeders began.

Big Boss was seen to dominate Plain. But now he began to pay visits to Wood. We caught him in the tunnel on a night when we had swung the doors so that they could not be pushed outwards, only inwards. (See Figure 8. We used by this method to trap these tunnels at approximately monthly intervals so as to check, weigh and examine any rabbit using them. Such handling always disturbed the rabbit psychologically.)

It was an opportunity to test what happened when a dominant buck was removed from his warren for a while, and isolated outside his normal territory.

Big Boss was in perfect condition, testes well down, his body fur glossy and unscarred by any recent fighting. He had maintained his position as head of Plain, and no doubt when caught en route for Wood had been seeking to extend the range of his proprietorship in that direction, or at least test its limits.

The tunnels were closed to prevent all further traffic between Plain and Wood, and Big Boss was released in Wood on October 29th, 1955. He was left in Wood for three weeks.

This experiment showed him to be deeply upset. To be handled by man, weighed in a cage, examined for parasites, and then released in unfamiliar territory from which there was no escape, was indeed a severe punishment.

Big Boss ran up and down alongside the netting boundary separating Wood from Plain. He was not observed to graze at all, but only indulge in this vain patrol, with at intervals frantic short bursts of digging – also in vain – at the base of the wire barrier. He was not seen to fight any other rabbit in B, but then he did not attempt, as far as our observations in daylight told us, to leave the boundary and approach the other inhabitants. Yet some fur lying alongside the fence suggested he had been involved in fighting.

This fur may not have been his. It could have been from the lone bachelor Timid Timothy, who had also been shut in Wood when we closed the tunnels. But knowing Big Boss from bitter experience in Plain, Timid Timothy kept out of his way (assiduously at first, our daily notes informed us) as the king buck made his fruitless afternoon, night and early morning patrol.

Timothy had found a new home under the Elm Tree Hide where he could be seen drowsing on a fine afternoon near a hole in the rotten heart-wood. He was to enlarge this and make it his permanent home in the coming months, until he was driven from it in due course by other home seekers in the expanding colony. Yes, the fur could have been his, torn from him by the impatient, anxious king Big Boss, or by the other two males in possession of territory in Wood; or it could have been Big Boss's fur, torn from him by the two dominant males of Wood.

Twenty-one days later, on a fine November afternoon, we reopened the tunnels to traffic, and Big Boss hopped back (thankfully we may suppose) towards his old home in the fine main ANE Burrow in the north-east portion of Plain.

What was his reception to be? Would his queen Beatrix remember and also accept him? What had been her behaviour during his enforced exile? Had she mourned his absence?

4 The Dynasty in Plain

The rabbit has a charming face;
Its private life is a disgrace.
I really dare not name to you
The awful things that rabbits do – ANON

The squealing scream of a rabbit in distress rang out – that heartrending cry of anguish which it utters when caught in a steel-jawed trap and which is so painful to the human ear because of its high pitch and human quality, like that of a child in the extremity of terror.

There was no doubt but that Big Boss was in such an extremity. He was being mercilessly attacked by Bold Benjamin who had usurped his throne, the comfortable quarters of the royal palace at ANE, and adopted his queen Beatrix.

It was as simple as that. Nature abhors a vacuum. The removal of the king (as we find it convenient to call the dominant male of the principal warren) from Plain to Wood had left the community in Plain without a leader. The next strongest male at once took up the coveted position. It was his right, of seniority, of might, of acquired experience. For Bold Benjamin was the only senior buck left in Plain. The rest were children of the year, under age, adolescent.

November, we were to find, was the season of final adjustment of the hierarchy. It was the season when the best winter quarters were acquired; there was a general move towards the driest, most commodious and deepest shelter which in the enclosures meant a knocking at the doors of the palace of ANE. Bold Benjamin had explored towards ANE in the absence of the king and found no opposition. He was even tolerated and finally welcomed by the grass widow, the queen Beatrix. Perhaps she was lonely for an adult male, since only young rabbits surrounded her? This could be, though no doubt we shall be accused of anthropomorphism if we insist that rabbits can feel lonely. We do not insist; we only know that rabbits enjoy company, that the female likes to and regularly does sleep with her mate throughout the year. She might therefore miss male company. Certainly the queen accepted the new consort swiftly.

Because of his dominance he was also accepted without question by the secondary does Bianca and Blanche as well as by the adult Skokholm does of the same age, Beautiful and Bronwen, which had come over from Wood during the neutral season of August and September, 1955, when the tunnels were first opened; and by the children of the year.

But his late mate, Bertha, remained at ASW where she had littered her families during the summer. She exhibited the conservatism and love of established home which proved characteristic in these studies of the mature female rabbit, as it is of many other animals, including man, where woman makes the home and usually does not wish to leave it unless compelled by necessity, by fear or other *force majeure*.

In the mellow light reflected from the trees by the setting sun the drama of the struggle between late king and would-be king was plain to the observer concealed in the Elm watchpost.

Bold Benjamin attacked Big Boss viciously a few minutes after the exile had run confidently into the underground palace. They met somewhere below. There was a thudding noise and they emerged together, rolling on the bare grass in a confused clinch. Separating, they leaped or pranced around each other for a few seconds, as if awaiting the moment to thrust home a telling bite or kick.

Then Benjamin darted in, bowling Boss over sideways, and sinking chisel-teeth into his neck.

Boss screamed, kicking out. Benjamin hung on, so that Boss half-dragged his enemy for a little distance before Benjamin lost or released his grip, tearing out as he did so a mouthful of Boss's fur.

Boss stopped screaming, ran away a few yards, then turned and rushed at Benjamin. A ragged edge of fur stood up on his neck, and already he seemed in a bad way. He had lost condition during his exile, and was psychologically as well as physically unfit for battle at that moment.

Benjamin, however, was on top of his form, exuberantly ready to defend his new position as dictator of the warren into which he had slipped so easily. He had enjoyed nearly three weeks of deputy kingship, of good living and lack of opposition from the inexperienced adolescent bucks.

The bucks grappled, each seeking to bite the head and neck of the other. They fell together sideways, bellies exposed, and scrammed with all four armoured legs.

Anyone who has handled a kicking rabbit without care will know how powerful the claws of the hind legs can be and how they rip the flesh; while the long teeth can inflict a deep wound with their double chisel action which can gnaw through the hardest timber.

The fighting rabbit with the strongest kick is likely to knock his opponent out, if not disembowel him altogether, unless his opponent turns away in time. The painful drumming on the belly and flanks threw up a cloud of white fur. Big Boss rolled away to save his entrails. But Bold Benjamin hung on to his neck with a locked grip of the teeth. Screaming fearfully the anguished Boss struggled free – at the cost of a severe wound at the base of his ears. He ran back towards the tunnels leading to Wood – at that moment the enforced exile he had experienced no doubt made Wood seem a place of comparative peace. In terror he sought to escape; but could not.

Shaking the fur of the ex-king from his mouth, the triumphant Benjamin hopped, stiff-legged and still threateningly, but no longer rapidly, towards Boss, who was now running along the netting boundary of the path dividing Plain from Wood, testing in vain the tunnel entrances which were closed.

The ex-king had had enough. He kept a healthy distance of several yards from Benjamin, running ahead when the new king ran, hopping more slowly when Benjamin hopped more slowly.

In this fashion, now fast, now slow, Benjamin pursued Boss up and down the length of the netting. As Boss dodged and ran hopefully towards ANE, Benjamin put on speed, intercepted and drove him fiercely back. As Boss moved away from his former palace ANE, Benjamin relaxed and dogged Boss in more leisurely fashion.

It was a serious chase, however, with an object in view. Doubtless it was motivated by instinctive sexual jealousy, and designed to ensure that Boss was either killed or rendered as thoroughly submissive as Benjamin had been in the past.

As it was getting dark it was not possible to follow the conclusion of the affair that evening. But next day Boss was still alive, but living in fear. All through the winter the ex-king lived as far away in Plain as possible, in the small box warren of ASW, where he mated with the stay-at-home Bertha, former wife of the new king Benjamin. The roles of the two oldest, dominant bucks in A were exactly reversed.

This was an artificial experiment which served its purpose. It indicated that the possession of a warren, when enjoyed for even a short period of time by a strong buck, gave him the confidence and courage to defend it with full vigour even against a larger buck who, returning as an absentee and with morale lowered by failure to dominate elsewhere, was psychologically ill-prepared to fight. As we have said, Big Boss was a mainland born buck and originally weighed half a kilogram heavier than Benjamin, but that physical advantage had been of no avail.

Boss seemed to recognise temporary defeat. He no longer came near ANE but remained quietly grazing around his new home at ASW. Here his new mate Bertha produced several litters in 1956, no doubt fathered by the ex-king.

The new king of Plain, Bold Benjamin, found himself master of a large settlement. Not only was he the consort of the old lady, mainland-born queen Beatrix, but under him were four does of the same age: Bianca, Blanche, Beautiful and Bronwen; three younger does, and three younger bucks (born in 1955) which inhabited the warren ANE.

To accommodate such a large family in ANE, large though this warren was, would have been impossible if the inhabitants had not extended it by driving underground shafts in all directions. These shafts were discontinued when wet ground was encountered; but uphill in the direction of ESL (Elm Stump Lodge, so called because it was first established by us as a shelter by burying an iron cistern, with holes, beside the stump of a felled elm of great age) the ground was dry. And in the autumn and early winter of 1956, shafts from ANE were linked up underground with ESL. The two warrens became one (Fig 9) and Bold Benjamin reigned as master and king of the whole of half-acre Plain.

He had much to do in the new breeding season. The old queen Beatrix remained his partner at the head of the warren. But Benjamin did not do much to help in the extensive excavations and improvements linking up ANE and ESL. Occasionally he was recorded as having a brief, fast, almost furious, spell at digging; he used his forepaws to cut out the soil and thrust it beneath his belly, heaping it between his hind legs, and backing out with it, his forepaws pressing the load together. At or near the entrance he would

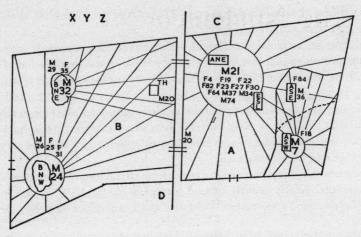

FIGURE 9. Warrens and territories of dominant bucks M 21 (Bold Benjamin) and M 24 (Bright Star), and of secondary bucks M 7 (Big Boss) and M 32 (Brown Boy), March, 1956

fling the soil backwards under his belly so that it spurted in a shower over the grass. He soon lost interest.

This was typical burrowing behaviour of the buck. The doe was much more industrious, and, using the same tools and technique, would work on for many minutes – in one instance more than an hour is recorded – appearing at intervals at the burrow entrance to push the earth outside, either with her chest frontally, but usually backing out with a load and flinging it clear with forepaws working beneath her belly. Digging burrows in spring was largely an activity of pregnant does; but digging also took place in the autumn, as soon as the ground was soft after rain, presumably to provide winter quarters for the enlarged colony.

Nest-making by the doe was rarely observed, because it seemed to take place at night; and the dominant doe in any case littered deep within the warren system. We found that she selected and dug out a new chamber there for each litter; and probably it was these nesting extensions to the main warren below ground which, as the growing kittens broke out to the surface, helped to link up ANE with ESL. Figure 10 shows the extent (ascertained by shaft-sinking and tracing with a pliant willow rod) of the doe Columbine's

PLAN OF COLUMBINE'S BURROW SYSTEM AT ASE

August 1957

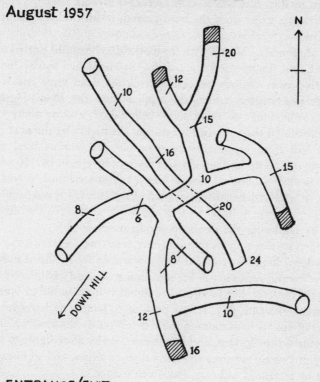

O ENTRANCE/EXIT

▨ NEST CHAMBER

0 1 2 3 4
FEET

Figures in burrow indicate approximate depth in inches from ground surface to floor of burrow (ascertained by sinking shafts at these points.)

Some exits are sites of earlier (closed) nest chambers.

FIGURE 10. Plan of Columbine's burrow system at ASE

home burrow system after two years of breeding. Only on four occasions were we able to watch the behaviour of a doe digging a nest burrow or 'stop' in the open by day. She was seen in each case to work near the edge of her grazing territory, away from the hard-grazed, much-trodden pasture of the main burrow.

On the afternoon of March 17th, 1956, the doe Beautiful started to dig on flat ground, and disappeared beneath in just about two hours. She paused only to drive away curious visitors. She carried dead grass and some live green vegetable matter, which she ripped from the base of grass tufts standing near by, and took them below before dusk, making many journeys. Evidently she lined the nest with fur during the night; by the next morning the earth had been replaced very smoothly and almost level with the surrounding turf. If we had not marked the spot by eye, in fact, it could have been overlooked as one of many bare, rabbit-scratched places in the enclosure, so well had Beautiful disposed of the excavated soil; this disposal is, of course, extremely important in the wild, to deceive the doe's many enemies, by rendering the nest-stop site inconspicuous.

We opened up this stop on that morning, and (two feet down the burrow, six inches deep) found four naked babies warm in the fur-lined nest; but in spite of our careful replacing of the nest-lining, fur and earth cover, the doe subsequently deserted her family. (We found it inadvisable to open a stop until about the seventh day. It was possible to handle and weigh week-old and older kittens without causing their desertion by the doe, although this clearly disturbed the kittens, and they were thereby more liable to leave the nest a day or two earlier than the normal three weeks, and were exposed to predation by buzzards and cats that much sooner.)

It was interesting to watch Beautiful's behaviour following our informative but otherwise unfortunate examination of her nest. The next day (after the nest-stop making) she did not go near the site by day, nor could we observe her appear to keep an eye on that area. It was as if she was making special efforts to avoid the smoothed-over site (both before and after we had opened and closed it) in order to keep it secret. On the third day, March 19th, the earth over the stop looked as if it had been disturbed, for it was no longer smooth; we realised, a few days later, that the doe had probably opened up the nest, smelled human scent or otherwise detected our visit, and without feeding the nestlings, roughly covered them up and deserted them. On the evening of March 20th we opened the nest to study progress, only to find the kittens cold and obviously dying.

Beautiful had meanwhile come into oestrus, and we saw her mate with the king buck Bold Benjamin two days after the birth of her litter. Buck and doe ran in circles for a few minutes, Beautiful flicking her tail high in the air as she made a kind of leaping dance at the same time. Suddenly she crouched down, paddling her hind feet backward to lift her hindquarters, her forelegs and breast pressed to the ground. Benjamin closed upon her, straddling her shoulders with his forelegs, and with rapid thrusting movements, the act of mating was completed. With a violent final ejaculatory thrust which lifted his hind feet clear of the ground, Benjamin arched his back and toppled over sideways, in an absurd, undignified manner, lay thus for perhaps one second, then broke loose from coitus. He returned to nudge Beautiful – who remained passive with lowered tail but apparently ready to copulate again. Benjamin, however, seemed prepared only to be affectionate, not to mate immediately. He remained close to her, licking her face at intervals; this action caused her to elevate her hindquarters for a few moments as if she expected him to mount again. But gradually the pair relaxed and rested for several minutes, before feeding was resumed, and it was soon too dark for us to see what happened next.

We have described the rabbit mating in detail because it was typical of rabbit copulation on the few occasions we observed it in nature; and it differs in no way from mating as observed in hutch rabbits. Sometimes the buck would mount again quickly and achieve another successful ejaculation, as indicated by his collapse sideways after. Sometimes the buck would mount and rest on the doe's back without a second, or third, mating. He occasionally pushed her around quite violently afterwards. Observers Myers and Poole state that 'When mating with young does the males were often heard to squeal in pain as they fell, and were seen to attack the female immediately with a vicious bite. Males did not appear to suffer any discomfort in mating with older females who had borne young before.' This suggests that the virgin doe, as is likely, has a narrow obstructed vaginal passage (as in the human virgin), which causes pain to the violently thrusting penis. One would have expected the virgin doe to feel pain; and in fact it is difficult for the human observer to be sure which of the pair is squealing! Certainly we have never been sure when listening to this 'consummation cry'. But usually the domestic buck in the hutch will grunt audibly after ejaculation in mating, as if in pain. In many species of mammal the female may be attacked after mating, and even bitten severely (e.g. in leopards I have observed in captivity) ; at least mammals do not eat their wives or husbands after! (We know that the female praying mantis and some female spiders devour the male after fertilisation, thus disposing of a now useless asset and enjoying a nutritious meal which contributes valuable protein to the developing ova fertilised by the male!)

Benjamin was seen to mate with Beautiful, but what about the other surplus does in the enlarged ANE (ESL)? Try as we might it was impossible to sort out the relationships here at all exactly. We could only observe that Benjamin, the king buck, dominated the whole of the enclosure Plain but we could not discover if he mated with any other doe than the queen. This was because mating was seldom observed; usually the rabbits grazed when they first appeared in the afternoon or evening, and they began to play more freely as darkness obscured them from the observer. In Australia observations in floodlit enclosures have revealed that mating takes place more freely after sunset, when intensive grazing is relaxed gradually as appetite is satisfied, and there is time to play.

King Benjamin doubtless did secure the surplus does for himself where possible, but we could not prove this; they may have been mated by the, other subordinate bucks, Careless, Crafty and Choosey (32, 37, 74), living with him in the ramifications of the huge central warren. We observed the king drive all other bucks out of his way when he made his daily round. Usually he returned afterwards and grazed in the vicinity of the queen Beatrix, and behaved as a courtier to her, protecting her, licking her face, mating with her.

It was noticeable that although he patrolled the south-western portion of the enclosure he did not spend more than a few minutes or sometimes seconds in that district. Having satisfied himself that the two subordinate pairs there remained subordinate, by the simple process of bullying them out of his path, he did not follow them underground. He quickly hopped back to the favourite grazing pastures of the queen. Here there was a more pressing patriarchal problem; the three bucks, Careless, Crafty and Choosey, were all in breeding condition in or around ANE and having intermittent games with eight fertile does of various ages. And lurking along the dividing fence was the outcast bachelor, Timid Timothy, who, as soon as the tunnels were open to traffic again (after a few weeks interval following the battle royal between the king bucks), appeared now in Wood and now in Plain, timidly sniffing on the trail of does grazing in his direction, and in any temporary absence of other bucks he flirted and played surreptitious sexual games with them.

King Benjamin, like many a royal master, found life full and demanding. He had to satisfy the sex requirements of his queen, and at the same time make sure no other male on his lands took liberties with his train of wife and concubines, at least not while he was in sight or knowledge of their actions. Clandestine flirtations between the sexes were many above ground, for rabbits obviously enjoy company, male with female; and that enjoyment is heightened or lowered by the degree of readiness of the female in her seven-day cycle to accept, and on one of the seven days even invite, copulation. As for male enjoying company with male, and female with female, this was sometimes apparent, especially in the neutral season, but usually they kept a little apart, a few feet – there was a minimum safety or 'individual' distance. Rabbits are essentially gregarious but not always sociable – their social structure is like that of a primitive community, which has its advantages in times of danger, as we shall see later.

To the human eye, each rabbit looks very much like the other; but it was quite obvious, in this study, that each rabbit knew the other rabbits around its territory as individuals, each with a personality and place in the hierarchy.

Observing the rules of minimum distance ensured that one rabbit did not take another by surprise. King Benjamin stalked through his subjects, dotted over the pasture at safe distances from each other, and all moved out of his way, some swiftly and submissively, others slowly and with a hostile raising of the hindquarters.

These hostile subjects were the older bucks and does who were second or third or otherwise high in the hierarchy of the royal court. They in turn dominated the younger and weaker rabbits around them. Their display or approach was sufficient to warn off the weaker individuals, but had no effect on the powerful king buck and quickly gave way to retreat on his appearance.

Thus a quiet and well-behaved society was maintained as soon as the order of precedence was established at the beginning of the breeding season, and the limits of territories of each individual ascertained. The importance of this peace, of the reduction of serious fighting to display and petty squabbles, is obvious in a large community, where fighting is a wasteful process and interrupts the development and prosperity of the colony.

Two strong males had not easily accepted the king's dominance, only submitting after direct fighting had resulted in defeat. These were the ex-king Big Boss, and the yearling Columbus (36). Each found a home for himself. Boss, as already described, lived with the new king's late consort Bertha at ASW. And in the indifferent warren – a couple of damp holes – at ASE, Columbus joined with his contemporary, Columbine (84).

As ASE was so damp, and seemed to us uncomfortable, we now improved it with a load of a ton of sand capped with a small corrugated roof eight by eight feet which gave the young couple dry quarters; and they reared several families therein during 1956.

The ex-king Big Boss, as he recruited his strength, as his wounds healed, frequently behaved as if he were trying out his prospects of regaining the kingship. This he did by easily dominating the younger buck Columbus in ASE. He pushed him around in the limited territory which the young buck occupied and grazed with his lady the young Columbine. As a result, this young pair were very restricted in their territory, the buck too timid to go far from home (Fig 9) and none too happy being bullied by the ex-king. In the following autumn he was to migrate to found a new home with a new mate in Wood.

Having secured his authority over all other rabbits which visited the south-west corner of Plain save the king buck himself, the ex-king grew bolder, and was seen to skirmish towards the centre as the spring of 1956 waxed and the young rabbits ran underfoot. He ignored, even tolerated, the small does; but moved closer and closer towards his former royal home. Was he seeking his old mate, the present queen?

But interest in territory was waning each summer day with the decline of fertility, and with the appearance of more young rabbits scampering about the whole enclosure. At last came the neutral season.

The ex-king Big Boss quietly re-entered his former palace.

There was no sign of resistance by any other male or female, and indeed no sign of king Benjamin.

Puzzled by this, on July 21st we opened up the burrows (this was an annual operation after breeding ceased) and verified that Big Boss was re-established at ANE. He had with him, not his former wife Beatrix (she had gone for ever – evidently she had died unseen of some cause unknown), but two does, Charmian and Christine (64 and 82), which had bred there under Bold Benjamin. Also in ANE were Columbus and several youngsters.

In ASE, her favourite and only domicile (1956–1958), we found Columbine with her latest family around her. Her mate Columbus, as above mentioned, was to desert her, and in fact was already on the move, and possibly seeking a better place. The interesting fact is that he had gone into ANE at about the same time as his superior Big Boss. But then, we repeat, this was the Neutral Season, when, their testes regressed and infertile, buck agreed with buck; and besides, ANE was so commodious now that there was room for many without overcrowding in the passages and parlours below ground.

The 1956 season nevertheless ended in a reversal of territorial positions between the two kings. Big Boss returned to dominate for a while the royal palace of ANE. And on opening ASW at this time we found Benjamin had returned and was living with his former (1955) mate Bertha and her latest family of three young 'kittens'.

As we needed some adult bucks for observation elsewhere we decided to remove the dominant king bucks Boss and Benjamin and study the struggle for dominance in the young secondary bucks.

After this the increasing colony in Plain received no further artificial manipulation; in the next two years it was allowed to build up to its maximum population undisturbed. What happened is described in Chapter 6.

5 The Kings of Wood

And rabbits scuttle through the maze of elfin paths –
FRANCES STEPHENSON: poem on Skokholm

What about the events in the enclosure Wood? We have heard little about this half-acre except to record the banishment of the king Big Boss there for three weeks and his subsequent return and battle with the usurper Bold Benjamin; and of the visits paid to Wood by the unfortunate skulking, mateless Timid Timothy.

Wood was furnished with a splendid dry natural warren BNW (i.e. Pen B, North-West warren) in the form of a bank of earth (originating in soil uplifted by the fall of an aged tree, decades ago, whose rotted remains we had removed). The wild population had died out from myxomatosis in 1954. Before that it had been a thriving colony, as could be seen from the several entrances, and the screen of nettles, burdock and comfrey around it, nitrogen-loving plants typical of ground dug and dunged over by numerous generations of rabbits.

Here, as already related, on June 22nd, 1955, was introduced a nucleus obtained from Skokholm: two adult bucks, Bright Star and Brown Boy; two adult does, Beautiful and Bronwen; and six young ones of the year. It was too late to expect them to breed, especially after the physical and psychological disturbance of catching and transhipping them from the fine sea-windswept salt pastures of an oceanic island, to the tree-bowered coarse grass of old parkland at Orielton. Bright Star was a big buck (as Skokholm bucks go) with a white mark on his forehead to give him further distinction. He appropriated the main warren of BNW at once and patrolled the pastures of all the half-acre during the first week. He chased his contemporary, Brown Boy, out of the way, and compelled the latter to live apart in the inferior and

Plate 1.
Doe rabbit grazing. The doe is the centre of the rabbit community, a matriarchy.

Plate 2.

Orielton House, east front. In the foreground Soay sheep grazing in Savanna (Pen C). Note meadowsweet behind wire-netting, in Plain (Pen A). Midsummer, 1958.

late 3.

abbit kittens, about nine days old, in nesting stop (opened up).

Plate 4.
The enclosures as seen from the house, Orielton.

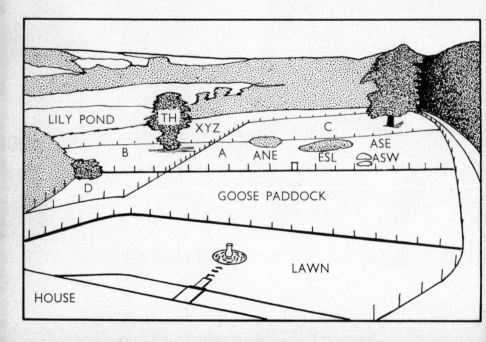

Plate 5.

Photograph and sketch plan of artificial underground warren.

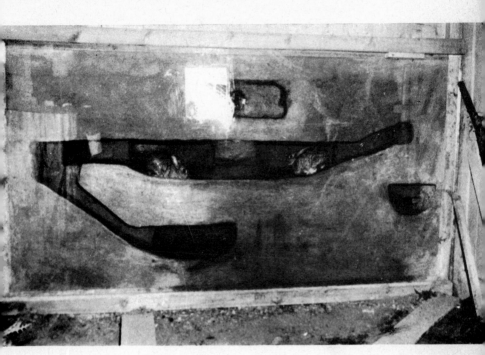

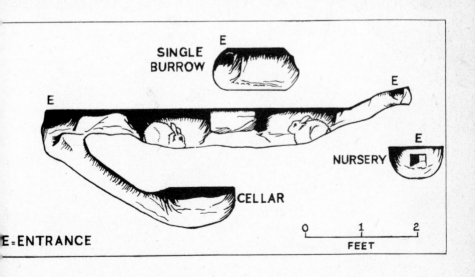

SINGLE
BURROW

E

E

E

NURSERY

E

CELLAR

E=ENTRANCE

0   1   2

FEET

Plate 6.
Rabbit family in the artificial warren.

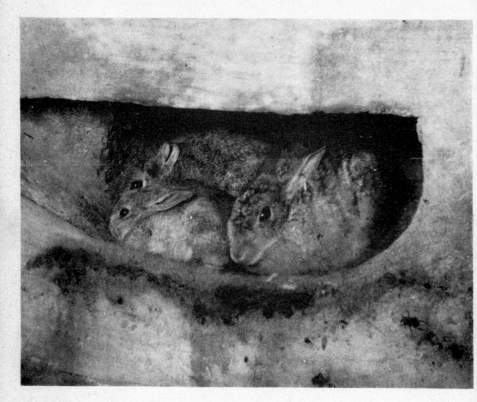

(Buck, with torn ear, at rear; doe, with tag in left ear, in front; half-grown rabbit, left front.)

Plate 7.
About five weeks old.

Plate 8.
Adult buck (marked nose) and immature rabbit.

often wet burrow at BNE. The two adult does settled with Bright Star at BNW, with the rest of the young ones.

We made a record of the patrolling movements of this dominant buck (24) three days after the introduction of the nucleus in Wood (page 45).

As it was the end of the season there was display but no fighting; and even this little territoriality waned and disappeared in July. There was a restless period, a neutral sorting out between the two half-acres, as soon as the two communicating tunnels were opened up for traffic at the end of June.

As already related, the adult does Beautiful and Bronwen crossed over to join the harem of king Benjamin in Plain, having in this neutral season not yet established a mating allegiance at home in Wood. They were to breed under the king Buck at ANE in 1956.

Five 1955-born Skokholm rabbits also settled in Wood. The Wood king, Bright Star, accepted into his superior warren BNW one young buck, Clansman (26), and two young does, Charity (25) and Cissie (31); while the secondary buck Brown Boy at BNE had the company of the young doe Clara (35) and the small young buck Chieftain (29) (who was therefore mateless – unless he could snatch his sex satisfaction on the sly).

This was the breeding nucleus in 1956, the king Bright Star with the white brow, dominating gently but firmly from October 1955 onwards all the half-acre Wood. By threat display he warned Brown Boy away from BNW; but he was not over-aggressive; and he permitted the third buck Clansman to live with a mate in the back passages of the royal warren. He appropriated as his queen, Charity; she was a few months older and more mature than the other warren doe Cissie, who lived with Clansman. It might be said – in anthropomorphic terms – that Bright Star was a model dictator, head of a benevolent autocracy.

In effect there were in the autumn of 1955 three mated pairs in Wood, and two unmated bucks: the youngster Chieftain at BNE; and the wanderer from Plain, the tunnel-dwelling timid old bachelor Timothy.

Brown Boy, boss of the small warren BNE, submitted to the king Bright Star in all situations and sites in Wood, except that we never saw the king enter the secondary buck's burrow. Territoriality was, as already seen in Plain, confined to the surface. But in his turn Brown Boy dominated the other males in Wood over that portion (Fig 9) of warren and pasture in which he lived, loved, moved and was permitted by the king buck to graze – the south-east quarter, which included the elm watchpost, under which in the spring of 1956 the lone bachelor Timothy sheltered and passed many skulking unrequited days.

The Wood king Bright Star led a dignified life, it seemed to us, observing him at close quarters from the tree hide. He was gentle but firm in his approach to other males during the breeding season. He displayed at them, and warned them off without fighting. His big frame (for a Skokholm rabbit) was what may have impressed them most. He was probably old physically but wily with experience. With his white brow he looked, and could well have been, several years old, perhaps at a very mature age for a wild rabbit, and past his prime, but at that time we had no means of recognising the age of a buck of over eighteen months, which was the moment when he reached full maturity and stopped growing.

His time had come however. He died in the autumn of 1956. Possibly he was beaten in a fight with the secondary buck Brown Boy who succeeded to the palace of BNW; possibly he died from heart failure, of old age, of failure to renew virility in time, even of chagrin. He died, that is to say he disappeared; but we did not find his corpse, nor do we know how it happened. The evidence of his demise became clear by degrees in the territorial struggle in the early winter of 1956–57. Brown Boy moved from the dismal damp quarters of BNE to the palatial BNW, leaving the inferior buck Chieftain in possession of BNE. Also his consort Clara remained at BNE; it was her breeding-ground and with female conservatism and despite the slummy wet burrow she resisted change. One of her daughters, Desdemona (42), remained with her, and paired (as we think) with a male of the same age, Desmond (41), possibly her brother.

The move into the royal residency by Brown Boy after the disappearance of the king Bright Star was greatly to his advantage. He acquired a dry and commodious warren with a ready-made queen, Charity; he became her consort, and by dominating the whole surface of Wood, he also acquired the kingship. In addition there were concubines to hand; the subordinate doe Cissie, whose mate Clansman had also died or been killed; and two 1955-born does, Caroline and Charmian (62, 64). Charmian was an emigrée from Plain.

Brown Boy reigned in 1957 over the four does, but he tolerated a young buck, who could have been his son, or the son of the ex-king, or of the

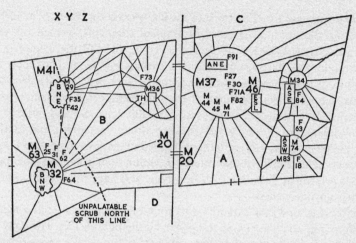

FIGURE 11. Warrens and territories of dominant and secondary bucks, April 1957

vanished Clansman, to live in the royal residency, and take as mate one of his retinue of does (Fig 11).

In the autumn reshuffle of 1956 the mature Charmian moved from ANE to settle permanently to breed in BNW. It was rare, in this study, for a doe to move from a warren once she had bred there. Also from half-acre Plain came the mature Columbus who had paired and bred at ASE in 1956. He had evidently been dominated and harried too often by the ex-king Big Boss during 1956 (page 58). He crossed over to Wood, deserting his mate Columbine, and there mated at TH with young Desirée who had enlarged the shelter under the elm watchpost used by bachelor Timothy. This pair settled deeper into the rotten heart of the elm, and were to live 'happily ever after' – that is, to be together in comparative peace and rear families in 1957 and 1958, with no other adults to bother them in this small new burrow.

Old bachelor Timothy was almost certainly born in 1953, possibly earlier. He was easily driven forth from the tree-hide shelter by the arrival of Columbus who came to protect young Desirée, who was responsible for digging new quarters there. Poor old Timothy had never been a success. It was surprising that he managed to go on living for we were to find that old displaced bucks died swiftly. But he was alive and skulking about the passage tunnels, now in Plain, now in Wood, well into the spring of 1957.

But his time was up. The story of his life, pieced together by us in little notes in our diaries, in a jigsaw of incomplete fragments, seemed sad, or at least unsatisfying. Whether he ever enjoyed to the full the virility of the mature male and its consummation in earlier seasons at Skokholm it is impossible to say; most likely he had, for he had been a fully developed two-year-old when first captured there and transported in March 1955; since which date he had been an outcast, unable to secure and settle in any warren with a doe. Timothy, as we have already reported, had at times flirted ineffectually on a fine afternoon with the ladies, young and old, along the edge of the territories of other bucks, or within them when the other bucks were not present to drive him off. But what had happened under cover of night was anyone's guess.

Exactly when and how Timothy died we never discovered – but sometime in the spring of 1957 he ceased to appear by the light of day. His body was found decaying in the tunnel on June 1st, 1957.

Now it was the turn of Brown Boy to meet his fate, he who had succeeded the aged Bright Star. He had achieved the kingship probably by fighting for it; although we recorded no physical fighting between these two, only display threats, serious fighting must have occurred at night – fur had been seen lying around in the dew of mornings in the late autumn of 1956.

A year later, in the late autumn of 1957, in his turn Brown Boy lost the kingship to the younger Skokholm buck Chieftain. Again, on these short autumn afternoons, there was little fighting to be seen; the rabbits often did not appear until dusk, and retired early in the dawn; but again the fur was flying around, and there were little cries and some loud screams to be heard from the enclosures on fine nights there, by the light of the moon or the stars.

Brown Boy fought long and hard, it would seem, before he submitted. But at last he was driven from BNW. Nor did he again control any other warren or woman although he crossed over to Plain, and was observed to run around there on two fine evenings. He was hounded away by the bucks, chiefs and subordinates, of which in the 1957–58 breeding season there were at least fifteen in the hierarchy of paired and virile bucks, with at least twenty fertile does in all Plain and Wood. He became an outcast; he skulked in the neutral ground between Plain and Wood, just as Timid Timothy had done.

We found the deposed Wood king Brown Boy sheltering in the tunnel passages by day, during November 1957. He was by now in poor condition, scarred from wounds about the neck and ears. Early in December he was very thin, his left ear had two-thirds cut off and missing. He was removed altogether, lest he die of persecution and misery in the now crowded, jostling communities.

Like the late king Bright Star, who had reigned two years before him, Brown Boy was a good age, at least four, possibly five years old, when we rescued him. He was, with the new king Chieftain, one of two bucks from the original introductions in 1955 to survive until the end of our study. He only continued to survive because we had succoured him.

Partly for sentimental reasons, partly for scientific reasons, we did not allow him to die a lingering, painful death as an outcast. We wanted an adult buck for another phase of our life-history study; we placed him alone in the small experimental pen D with its artificial underground observation chamber. Here, he gradually recovered his health, protected from the attacks of the king Chieftain by the wire-netting fence dividing Wood from D (Fig 12). And, to restore him completely, as soon as he showed signs of

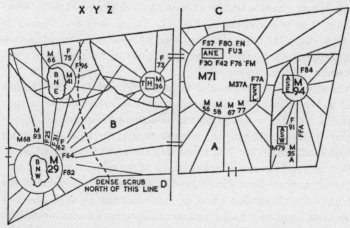

FIGURE 12. Warrens and territories of dominant bucks M 29 (Chieftain) and M 71 (Daredevil), and of secondary bucks (three smaller circles), March 1958

restlessness, by his patrolling of that fence, we gave him a young wife. We made amends in this way, and it pleased us to see him happy and dominant once more.

Figures 6, 9, 11 and 12 show the layout of warrens and territories of the dominant and secondary bucks in the four seasons over which the study extended.

In the first year of low population the leading or king buck in each half-acre dominated the whole ground in that half-acre with ruthless despotism of tooth and claw. But in the second year, with already sixteen adults competing for the grazing of the higher, drier, sunnier, more popular enclosure Plain it was difficult for one buck to cover this half-acre authoritatively. We have seen that the king Bold Benjamin, having driven out the old mainland-born dominant Big Boss and banished him to the secondary inferior warren ASW, had his time strenuously occupied. After his signal battle with Big Boss he did not press his victory too far; he was too occupied nearer home in controlling the four young bucks secondary to him. Figure 9 shows that although he kept his control, by March 1956 he had ceased to patrol the far south-west corner where the deposed Big Boss lived quietly with one doe.

In Wood, with but seven adults (including Timothy) to dominate in 1956, old king Bright Star – notably easy-going and gentle though firm – had experienced a year of comparative peace. He had had no difficulty in sub-duing those subjects over the two warrens and all the surface of the half-acre – they had plenty of room to get out of his path, twice as much *lebensraum* as the inhabitants of Plain.

But the advent of a new couple, displacing Timothy at TH (the tree-hide warren) in Wood and the presence altogether of twelve adults in 1957, had reduced the effective range of control which could be covered by the king (now Brown Boy) and again the farthest corner, the south-east corner, had to be neglected. Brown Boy had mostly left this corner and its rabbits alone – we never recorded his presence south-east of the tree hide.

In this chapter we have shown how Brown Boy was deposed in his turn, by the virile Chieftain. But when he came to reign in 1958 this new king Chieftain was head of a half-acre containing even more subjects (thirteen) including five potent and aggressive bucks ever ready to dispute his kingship. Wisely he did not seek to stray far in asserting his authority. Home matters were more important this year. He hardly ever visited the territory TH of the south-east corner, where Columbus was mated with Desirée. Nor did he assert himself more than casually at the warren BNE, where two breeding couples lived rather bickering lives in this poor damp dump of a burrow.

Chieftain was at last in this coveted hard-won position (he had for two years lived as secondary buck) as head of the clans in Wood. He spent most of his fertile season in managing the tricky problems of the palace and demesne of BNW. Here his queen and favourite in this first and last year of his kingship was the 1955-born Charity; and in addition there was the secondary doe Cissie of the same age. Both these does had come as young virgins from Skokholm, and had retained their original positions of queen and second lady in Wood from the start to the finish of our study. Chieftain was thus living with his contemporaries from Skokholm, the two middle-aged ladies, who, like the majority of women the world over, loved, lived and stayed at home, in this case with little discomfiture considering it was the royal palace of the half-acre Wood, a pleasant enough place for a rabbit with its shady scrub of nettles, its garden of comfrey, ragwort, burdock and other tall weeds.

What did these old island-born rabbits think about when on fine after-noons in the warm spring of 1958, they took their ease together in the sun and shade of the royal palace? Something must have stirred in their brain? The impulse to live was strong yet in these Skokholm-born ladies of the court of this Skokholm-born king. They lived by impulse, like many animals: on impulses from the brain they hopped from their burrows, washed themselves, preened, grazed, skipped skittishly out of the king's way or flirted or allowed him to mount them. They ate much of the time, for the pasture was poor and over-grazed by now, and lacked quality, they dozed and sunbathed. In other words they thought with a rabbit's intelligence of what they would do next, in any situation, upon any stimulus received from around them. This 'intelligence' advised them to do pleasant things, to avoid doing unpleasant things.

When they saw the buck Brown Boy hop up to the netting dividing Wood from Pen D did they recognise their former king? If they knew their present king Chieftain so well, accepted him, approved his protection, loved him (at seven-day intervals, completely) surely they recognised the ex-king with whom they had mated, by whom they had had many children but a year ago? For it is evident that rabbits do recognise each other, as friend, foe, enemy, or neutral, male or female.

Is that why they sometimes, indeed quite often, went close to the netting and appeared to touch noses through the meshes with their late husband? Is that why Brown Boy ran up and down the foot of the netting so much that he wore a path quite bare there in the spring of 1958?

Secure in Pen D, Brown Boy was well fed and enjoying normal sexual cohabitation alone with his young, year-old wife. But still he hankered after something else, something which made him try to get through the wire barrier, as if he would be closer to these ex-wives of his, and offer them love again? Or was he spoiling for a renewal of the fight with the king buck?

The king buck was not so occupied with the bucks and does accessible to him in Wood that he could or did ignore the reappearance of the deposed Brown Boy in Pen D – which was a threat to his kingship. At first he frequently ran up to the netting and leaped at it, vainly trying to attack the ex-king on the other side, as if to renew the severe punishment which he had but a few weeks before inflicted. And the old king on these occasions would usually retreat a little way, and crouch down, laying flat his one and one-third ears. But as soon as the king had gone, the ex-king would hop back to the netting and sit down quietly, perhaps hoping for another little conversation with his ex-wives, who perhaps did not despise or hate him but were only curious, and perhaps ready, on suitable 'days of attractiveness' to submit to him.

This picture of nostalgic longing between rabbits is, you will say, ridiculous. We quite agree that we have been a little sentimental here. We should perhaps have used the words 'recrudescence of vigour, increased androgen secretion' as being more scientific. Well, let us stick to the facts and leave the question marks where they belong.

The facts are that the ex-king did voluntarily visit the dividing fence at intervals all day long while he was above ground, to gaze and sniff at the ladies whom he had once loved (mated) and whose grazing ground adjoined his; and if they were not co-operative (and most of the time they were too busy about their domestic duties of feeding and breeding) he would rest with one side against the netting, fur pushed through, and stare or doze indolently at his ease, belly full. Of course this was not the whole of his life. He grazed a lot, he studied his accessible young mate by following her around as she grazed, he played with her. But always he came back to the dividing fence. Here, too, he deposited pellets – a sizeable latrine.

A simple and acceptable hypothesis could be that he was continually on guard there, at the unnatural, enforced but nevertheless effective, limit of his present territory; that he was making a gesture of the male – futile, yet a challenge, as far as it went. To that we might add the observation that we found in this study that the rabbit is as curious and as stimulated by the actions of their own species as any other animal with a mammalian brain, including man. We suggest that Brown Boy, like a husband temporarily tired of the too soothing company of a compliant wife, liked watching the events of the crowded compound of Wood. They stimulated him. Moreover there was nothing, and certainly no other rabbit, to stop him from enjoying this innocent satisfaction of his natural curiosity. He was master of his own territory again, psychologically a reasonably balanced rabbit, with an impregnable if unnatural barrier along a territorial demarcation line almost as invisible as those, inside the enclosures, which he had known in his days as a secondary buck, and bounded on the outside by exactly the same artificial limits (wire netting) as when he was king buck.

Chieftain grew used to the inexplicable presence of the ex-king sitting or strolling so inaccessibly on territory too near to the royal palace ever to be acceptable to a top buck. By trial he had learned that when you leaped at the old buck you were bounced back uncomfortably by this curious transparent barrier as if the old buck had butted you. So he desisted at last, mostly using threat displays if he happened to register the presence of Brown Boy on his rounds in that direction. There was more satisfaction in chasing and putting to flight the accessible bucks in the enclosure. But perhaps he was not an excessively jealous buck – there was little need to be. After all there were five fertile does in his palace, enough to satisfy his vigour at intervals, and only two young bucks besides himself to meet their sex requirements. At least one of the surplus does was his, but what was his relationship with the other three?

We never completely worked out the relationships of the secondary rabbits which went on behind the tall weeds here, but suspect, from the field records of their movements, that the two other males, born only a year before and not fully adult, although fertile, were paired with the two youngest females. This would have been normal, but we were not able to prove it. This was a year of congestion, and pressures, and confusion among the inhabitants of the over-populated enclosures, which made it difficult for us to be sure of the meaning of all the recorded movements of the more skulking secondary characters.

6 Over-populated World

*A number of rabbits, which possessed
all the hillocks and dry places* – GILBERT WHITE OF SELBORNE

We have finished with our tale of the dynasty of the kings of Wood. Now we must finish with the events in Plain, already troubled by problems of over-population.

Enclosure half-acre Plain was more open, a savanna with more palatable grazing pasture than in Wood, although they were equal in size: 2,420 square yards each. But the northern one-third of Wood had been a weedy area at the start of our study and its warrens there partly covered with rhododendrons and the litter of a huge, long, decayed, uprooted tree; in order to see the rabbits easily we had cut down these rhododendrons and most of the tree rubbish, and removed the trash before the introduction of the nucleus in 1955, but in the subsequent years the rhododendrons and tall unpalatable weeds re-grew abundantly and advanced over the grass, encroaching on the grazing to the south. Rabbits are ever despoilers of grassland.

Enclosure half-acre Plain had no old bush growth. Its whole surface was open, though it became more weedy with meadowsweet, nettles and ragwort as the increasing stock of rabbits ate out the nutritive grasses, leaving the turf more impoverished each year. But because of its higher, drier, situation and above all its greater grazing area it could support (and therefore attracted) more rabbits to live and to breed there.

At the end of Chapter 6 we reported the removal of the two warrior bucks who, both kings of Plain in turn, were required for study elsewhere; and by the removal from the hierarchy of the king and second buck respectively the kingship of Plain was left vacant for whosoever might take it over.

Columbus had fled across to Wood (possibly encouraged to go by our handling of him in the warrens when we had removed the kings). That left only three proved fertile bucks, Careless, Crafty and Choosey, born in 1955, breeding in 1957, in Plain, together with their sons the young bucks born in 1956. Many of the young rabbits had disappeared at a tender age, some taken by predators, but of the survivors there lived to the fertile stage five young bucks (44, 45, 46, 71 and 83). These were identified during the late winter and early spring as having become secondary bucks and subservient to the three older bucks (Fig 11).

Crafty, born in Plain in 1955, assumed the kingship thereof in the spring of 1957. He dominated and dwelled in the palace of ANE. The old queen Beatrix was dead (how she died no one knows; she was believed to be only middle-aged – she might have been senile, however). Crafty found himself consort to the eldest surviving female, Bronwen (born at Skokholm in 1954 or earlier). Under them in ANE were four young bucks born in 1956, the 1955 Skokholm-born doe Cheerful (who might have been his second lady or concubine) and three young does born in 1956. The sexes were now equal in numbers in the combined warren ANE–ESL, as they were in fact in the whole of Plain – if we except the outcast bachelor Timothy, wandering between Plain and Wood.

Choosey was petty chieftain of ASW and, of equal age and almost equal strength with the king Crafty, he dominated a goodly corner of Plain, as Fig 11 illustrates. And, with him, for by now ASW had been enlarged to accommodate two pairs of rabbits, was his mate the old 1953-born Bertha, ever faithful to her home warren; and a young subordinate couple born in 1955.

At ASE lived another female faithful to her burrow, Columbine, born in 1955, who had been adopted by the buck Careless, also born in 1955, but who had lived for a year in ANE under the kingship of Bold Benjamin in 1956. He was therefore like the other master bucks two years old when he carved out a territory for himself and his doe in the sand-topped warren of ASE.

'Carved out' was the appropriate description in this season. There were seventeen adult rabbits frequenting the half-acre Plain in the spring of 1957. The pressure for living space had been already severe in 1956 (seventeen breeders in that spring too) but by 1957 the pasture had deteriorated farther. Sweet grasses and clovers had virtually disappeared, and the cowslips and primroses, beautiful to look at but unpalatable to eat, had spread considerably over the close-grazed turf. Conditions of bare pasture suited the primulas; and they greedily stole more of the surface early in spring with their broad rosettes of leaves pressed to the ground, obliterating weaker species.

The three dominant males fought much over the establishment of territories. Although Crafty could be said to be king, secondary bucks Careless and Choosey this season each fought off the king buck and the other secondary buck when these came over the invisible barrier around their warrens (Fig 11).

Fur lay round Plain every morning, newly torn during these boundary disputes, during the late winter and early spring. Tension was mounting as competition for living (breeding and feeding) room increased. It seemed as if the maximum breeding population had been reached – eight pairs to half an acre; as if $\dfrac{16}{2420}$ square yards = approximately 150 square yards of grazing to one adult rabbit was the limit, and by no means adequate for their comfort and happiness. The three dominant bucks inhabited and shared Plain by an armed truce, observed only so long as each did not invade the other's territory.

The testes of the young males at six months of age in Plain in the autumns of 1956 and 1957 were not visible when we examined them in the annual round-up at that season. In these autumns the testes were slow to descend from the abdomen and enter the scrotal sac. These young bucks could not therefore have copulated successfully and achieved fertile unions with does in the early winter. But the scrotal sacs of the older males were well filled out in October, and they may have mated with both old and young does which were then ready. Their dominance was associated with this development of their testes before that of the adolescents.

Nevertheless, although mating was recorded from November onwards, we saw no young weanling rabbits above ground in Plain or Wood before early March. Yet mainland rabbits born in the freedom of the wild, produced weanlings even in November.

What had happened to the litters (if conceived) from matings in the winter? Had they been born and abandoned by the doe for lack of milk?

But we had found no evidence of nest-making before March.

The majority of does were, of course, from Skokholm. We had lived twelve years on that island and knew from experience of observing as well as handling hundreds of rabbits there that few young rabbits appeared before April, although mating occurred and females were occasionally found to be pregnant when killed on the island in late winter. Perhaps these Skokholm-born rabbits and their progeny born at Orielton were following the inborn insular pattern fixed by generations of living under tough winter conditions.

Some desperate fights were witnessed in Plain during the spring of 1957. We shall describe that between two secondary bucks which resulted in the death of the defeated.

The yearling bucks were not in first full breeding condition until March and April; this made them at that time restless, aggressive and on the search for sexual and territorial adventures. The scent glands on the chin developed and exuded droplets which matted the fur on the chin into a little streaky beard. They defended their doe if they had achieved one, or sought for one if they had not. They defended their territory around their burrow if they owned one; and they marked this ground deliberately with droplets of strong-smelling chin scent, and – more unavoidably – with urine and pellets.

On the evening of April 28th the yearling buck Daredevil (71) had been feeding towards the south-west corner of Plain, along the fence and just within the large territory held by the king Crafty, under whose dominion he was, to whom he submitted, and by whom he was thereby indirectly protected. Indeed, the king could have been his father for all we knew (although we did not know); both had been born in Plain.

Daredevil may have been merely seeking fresh pasture on the edge of his normal grazing territory, or may have been looking aggressively for a fresh doe when he wandered off the king buck's domain and into the far corner of Plain where lived two pairs of rabbits at ASW. He 'chinned' the grass there and laid his scent. As it happened, the older master buck of ASW, Choosey, was not in view; but the younger subordinate buck Diehard (83) was present, grazing near his doe (63).

As soon as Daredevil moved towards the peacefully grazing doe her body-guard Diehard hopped stiff-legged in display to meet the trespasser. In reply Daredevil broke the rules of territory by meeting and circling around him stiff-legged and ready for a trial of strength.

The outraged Diehard forthwith ran head down at Daredevil, who neatly dodged him. After another round or two of displaying in evasive circles the intruder retired towards his own, the main, warren. Peace was restored by this display ceremony, and wasteful fighting avoided. Diehard saw the visitor off to the edge of his land and beyond, in fact out of his territory almost up to the burrow at ESL. He then retired home to ASW, perhaps a little too pleased with himself.

This apparent surge of new confidence in himself, this cocksureness in his success as a virile male which had enabled Diehard to see a rival buck out of his territory and well into that of the rival was utterly defeated next day. We chanced to be on watch when he was seen to hop out of his own territory around ASW and advance as he had yesterday right up to the warren at ESL. Suddenly Daredevil appeared from a burrow close to the trespasser and after a moment's sniffing in the direction of Diehard suddenly and violently attacked him. He got his teeth into Diehard's back and hung on. He had completely surprised the intruder.

The pair rolled on the ground, and fearful screams arose. It was impossible to follow exactly what was happening or which buck was screaming for a moment as they rolled and tumbled over the surface of the main warren, ANE–ESL. They bit and kicked in a close mêlée, lying sideways, bellies together.

Then Diehard broke away. He appeared to be crippled, as if Daredevil had cut the tendons of his hind legs – as if he had been hamstrung. He seemed incapable of swift retreat. He dragged his hind legs with a swaying motion as if they were paralysed from rump to toes.

Daredevil leaped on him, biting at his shoulders now. With a long quavering scream Diehard crawled into the nearest bolthole, one of several around ESL. Daredevil remained outside, shaking fur from his jaws, preening himself.

On the third day, at about 17.50 hours, on April 30th, we noticed Diehard crawl out of a burrow in ANE and stagger along the fence south-eastwards, as if avoiding the scene of his defeat at ESL, as if trying to get back to his home at ASW by a roundabout way. His hind legs were useless. He collapsed behind some dead weeds in the south-east corner. He was found dead a few days later beside the wire-netting near his own burrow.

This was the beginning of dominance for Daredevil who became king of the overcrowded community of Plain in 1958.

The late summer of 1957 brought on an early neutral season, an earlier end to the breeding than usual, a shortening doubtless due to the stresses of overcrowding. Eight does had littered between them possibly $8 \times 12 = 96$ live kittens; but the majority had been lost to predators at the weanling age.

The hardships of winter that followed brought further mortality. An epidemic of coccidiosis broke out. Most of the bucks which had been breeding in 1957 died in this winter. The ex-king, Crafty, died; so did the secondary dominant bucks, Careless and Choosey.

By the turn of the year the new king of Plain, Daredevil, was master of the survivors – nine does and five young bucks. Of these all were under a year old except the 1955-born doe Cheerful, who now by order of seniority became his queen: and also the 1956-born doe Desdemona, who had – a rare event – changed her breeding-ground by migrating from Wood to Plain to join his retinue; probably she had moved because the pasture in Wood was even less palatable than the poor grazing in Plain.

Daredevil had no rival all winter in Plain. But at the turn of the year, and early in February, it was noticeable that a year-old buck (94) was dominating the south-western quarter of Plain. He had settled at ASE with the old 1955-born Columbine, who had thus bred in this warren for her third season. By March he was in full possession of this quarter territory of Plain, and was seen to dominate two young couples in occupation of ASW (Fig 12).

The yearling buck stood on his home ground and displayed at the king Daredevil, master of the other three-quarters of Plain. And Daredevil, perhaps remembering certain unsuccessful adventures in the SW corner in 1957, left him alone – Daredevil already had a comfortable retinue of queen and concubines (if we may use such a term) subservient to him in the royal palace of ANE–ESL.

7 Hard Times

The conies are but feeble folk,
Yet they make their houses in the rocks – AUTHORISED VERSION

The preceding chapters have covered the observed behaviour of marked individuals over some 1,300 hours of patient watching from the tree-hide in the decayed elm. It was not always as easy as it may appear on paper. The hide was in shade, often cold and usually draughty. There were days of high wind and rain when the elm quivered and swayed and the corrugated iron roof creaked incessantly or rain beat a merciless tattoo, and it was impossible to hold binoculars and telescope steady enough to read the numbers on the eartags of the individual rabbits. Many times occurs the entry in the log: 'U.R. buck (or doe) behaving . . .' U.R. = rabbit with unrecorded number.

Sometimes the eartag numbers were temporarily obscured by dirt acquired in wet weather underground. But the rabbits' sex was known because males were tagged in the right, and females in the left, ear. Buck and doe can sometimes be recognised by the broad powerful squat head of the male rabbit which contrasts with the long refined greyhound head of the female – but it is not an infallible distinction. The king buck was recognisable by his lordly behaviour and confident bearing on patrol of his territory. Some rabbits had a white mark of varying size on the forehead, or a paler or darker pelage, a ragged or torn ear, a spot bare of fur, especially on rump or forehead and probably due to fighting or claw scratching at close quarters underground.

These minor wounds became increasingly common in the last two crowded years.

There were many hours of watching when few rabbits appeared in the hours of daylight; or when if they did appear the foul weather made accurate tag-reading impossible. We never discovered why rabbits were slow to appear on a few of those days when the weather appeared ideal for them and for us: calm, sunlit afternoons would, however, normally bring us both out early. Like humans, they loved to bask in the warmth of the sun, lying on one side with their hind legs stretched out to the heat, the white belly and scut conspicuous, their eyes blinking and sometimes quite closed. Rain troubled them less than it troubled us. They did not like rain, but would graze through a light storm when hungry. Wind did not bother them at all.

In the late summer and autumn it was essential to capture and mark all likely survivors from the spring litters. This was done by pulling them out by hand from the nest-steps where they were born; or by catching them with long-handled nets as they lay out in 'forms' or 'squats' in the long grass – which so many young ones would do in the summer; by running them into burrows over which purse-nets had been placed; and the balance of un-marked youngsters would be rounded up at the annual opening of the burrows in August.

(The number of the ear-tags of the rabbits as quoted in the preceding chapters may seem erratic as if they did not follow a regular system. But we had begun with the figure 1 and continued up to 99, as well as using a few letters. Rabbits with numbers not quoted in these studies all died soon after marking and are therefore included collectively in our records in the unimportant class of also-rans, referred to as 'other rabbits' including especially 'young rabbits'. But in order to avoid using a third numeral on the ear-tags, which would have made it necessary to paint three small figures on the tags instead of one, or two, large ones, and so made reading from a distance more difficult, we later freely re-employed tags taken from the ears of young rabbits which had been found dead and therefore had no history worth an individual case-record. This explains the apparently random sequence of numbers, of eartags of low denomination on the ears of rabbits born in the later years of our study.)

Early in the spring the daffodils, planted down the centuries by the Knights and Ladies Owen who had made Orielton the gracious place it is, grew up tall and elegant like ladies themselves, embellishing the bare-bitten surface of the enclosures. Our rabbits did not eat daffodils. Nor, even in the spring hunger after their winter of discontent (overcrowding, malnutrition) would they touch the arum or lords-and-ladies which opened spatulate sheath to reveal the bitter-tasting red fruit wattle. They left certain flowers and leaves severely alone: cowslip, primrose, rhododendron, burdock, comfrey, sorrel. They would nibble a little young stinging nettle in their hunger, and even the sour-tasting leaves of red campion were mown down over the winter.

The untouched burdock, comfrey and nettle grew tall and rank each summer, invading, shading and destroying more and more of the pasture. It provided cover for the rabbits who would sit in its shadow for periods varying from a few seconds to an hour or more. Here a rabbit was at ease; it would doze, scratch, preen, yawn, 'swallow the cud' or merely sit perfectly still.

It was not that there was not enough to eat in the two enclosures, Plain and Wood, there was always something to eat. The long periods when rabbits sat in the open doing nothing indicated that they were not starved. As we had the power to control them it would have been cruel to have starved them. Overcrowded human populations, in India and China, and in city slums elsewhere, can always eat something – and in some primitive tribes in times of scarcity humans will eat earth in order to fill their bellies. They are perpetually hungry but not starving.

Like those dense human populations the rabbits were not eating food sufficiently nourishing to keep them in perfect health. But some, the dominant or ruling class, again as in human communities, were enjoying, by right of their occupation of the best positions (the best warrens and grazing ground) the best of the available food supply. The secondary and lower individuals in the hierarchy had to be content to feed on poor pasture on the fringes of the dominant's territory, or poach on that territory when the dominant was not present.

The whole of our detailed notes of movements of marked individuals in the latter part of the year 1957 and 1958, when Plain and Wood were full with the young of the year, confirmed this structure of priority of the ruling bucks and does to have and to hold.

'To the rich shall be given riches, but the poor shall be made poorer.' The weaker rabbits suffered for being weak; they were weak because they had not been brought up in the benefits of living under the king in the protection of the royal palace. They could be driven by the king and his family from the little patches of delicious white clover and grass still surviving here and there, but grazed daily in the flush season until the very roots were eaten out and nothing green was left. The weak nibbled here and there, where they could find a corner to live, momentarily unmolested. And they would dig around succulent stems and eat them down below ground level.

But to this handicap of being born inferior and suffering banishment from a seat at the superior table, was added another, more subtle disadvantage - an inferiority complex.

Rabbits are as full of moods as humans are, or any other advanced species of mammal. They are extremely sensitive to visual impressions. They respond to a display of *joie de vivre* in a neighbour who jumps into the air of a fine afternoon, for they will do the same. They are intensely interested in watching sexual activities, and are stimulated thereby to behave sexually too. They observe a fight with curiosity, and are ready to fight themselves if there is a prospect of winning, even to sham fight and then run away if in danger of losing.

We have seen that out of fighting at the commencement of the breeding season emerges an ordered society with every buck and doe aware, by trail and error, of its position in the hierarchy. The lowest members were not badly off in the first two years of enclosure life, for then there was enough *lebensraum* of food and shelter for all. But in the last two years at Orielton there was not; and territorial pressures were such that every day and night there were skirmishes and bickering, leading to a state of stress in the lowermost ranks that could easily be described as an inferiority complex. In human beings a sense of inferiority results in varying degrees of metabolic derangement; and in extreme cases causes a change in adrenal functions affecting the health of the patient, even his sanity and will to live. (And in women it may result in sterility, or, if pregnant, miscarriage.) The feeling of inferiority resulting from persecution by dominant rabbits led to what seemed to be an almost complete failure of the younger subordinate does to produce live young in 1958. We recorded these subordinate young does present, old enough to breed (they had been born in the 1957 spring) but without signs of producing live young. These does (FFA, F7A, FM, FN, FU3 – see Fig 12) may well have mated, but if so the young may have been 'resorbed' (i.e. re-absorbed without abortion) before parturition; or possibly the fertilised ova failed to mature.

Observing rabbits in similar small enclosures in Australia, Mykytowycz

(1958–61), considers that in dense populations the stress associated with subordinate status is probably the major cause of what is known as resorption or prenatal mortality. He found that both dominants and subordinates shared in the increased prenatal mortality, but that the older females, as dominants, produced more live young, that is completed more pregnancies, than subordinates.

Although we could not afford to kill our young does in order to test them *post mortem* for evidence of prenatal mortality, their failure to produce live young seems explicable, in the light of Mykytowycz's observations, as *stress*: stress through friction and fighting between females, through harrying of females by males, and through competition for a food supply already deteriorating through over-population.

It is these factors, we believe, that may have triggered off resorption on a larger scale in the last spring and summer in the enclosures where we estimated that only about one hundred young had been born to the twenty-four does present in December 1957. If, as we believe, few of those does born in late spring in 1957 produced young in 1958, then the production of live kittens by the remaining adult and older does was still very low. Of the estimated hundred kittens in 1958 only thirty-four survived to be marked with eartags in July.

When the enclosures were disbanded in December 1958 there were still fewer surviving. Conditions were decidedly uncomfortable; and it was time to conclude the experiment.

Had the enclosures been maintained, and the survivors permitted to breed, what would have happened?

We believe that the older does would have occupied the dominant queen positions, as we had seen them do in the preceding seasons, and would have bred with greater success (that is producing more live young) than the subordinate does. The latter, mostly if not all under one year old in December, would not have come into breeding condition before March or April. They would mate with fertile bucks but there would be few if any live births; the resulting pregnancies would be terminated at half-term by the process of resorption of the foetus. The young does would mate again and again, as long as the season of libido of the males lasted, conceive, and re-absorb the resulting developing ova or embryoes.

The phenomenon of prenatal or intra-uterine mortality known as resorption, in which little or no abortion occurs, is now known in a number of animals under stress of over-population. It is a useful device, a form of self-limitation or birth control, a self-regulating fecundity mechanism operated by density factors producing degrees of stress.

The conditions arrived at in the Intensive Acre Plain–Wood are, in fact, an indication of what may happen on many small islands where populations of sheep, rabbits, rats or mice are uncontrolled by man, although originally introduced by him deliberately or by accident. On Skokholm Island the rabbit population builds up to a maximum density like that reached in Wood and Plain at Orielton. The weaklings are killed off by disease and predators. Only the strong middle-aged rabbits (eighteen months old or above) survive the winter in a fat condition. All the rabbits under one year old are found to be very thin and in poor condition on the island throughout the winter, but if they survive they begin to put on fat with the summer flush of grass and in their turn become dominants. But these young does may very well fail to breed – Hugh Lloyd tells us that they rarely have more than one litter of live young under crowded conditions, and until they are over their second winter, and become 'queens'.

When conditions on small islands have resulted in a very high climax population and are followed by a severe winter, there is bound to be severe mortality; and this is known as a 'crash'.

Students of factors governing the levels of animal populations are not yet agreed on what physical processes determine precisely the 'crash' of a maximal population. The simple answer of overcrowding, leading to disease and starvation, which appeals to the layman as the obvious explanation, is not altogether acceptable to the biologist seeking a true understanding of what appears to be a complex situation of physiological and psychological pressures. By restricting a multiplying population of rabbits at Orielton to one acre we were offering to the inhabitants what one scientist elsewhere has called, dramatically, 'physiological insult'.

We had not, however, pursued the experiment to an actual 'crash'. The overcrowding had proceeded so far as to inhibit much further increase of numbers. Studies of the sudden eruption and emigration of lemmings in Scandinavia suggest that when these creatures build up numbers (by breeding under the snow in early spring and then again in summer) to 'crash' point, there is a general lowering of resistance to parasites and disease due to overcrowding discomforts (rather than food shortage) and, above all, to severe psychological tension. This results in endocrine malfunction or 'imbalance'. The population is highly nervous and at last suddenly takes flight in a panic emigration in which most of the travellers die. Few remain – but still a few do – to build up numbers again in the ancestral territory; and in due course, another explosion and emigration occurs, following a somewhat irregular 'cycle' of years.

Studies of wild animals in artificial enclosures are admittedly artificial, but not altogether unnatural if the conditions of range and food supply are reasonably adequate; and ours at Orielton resembled the conditions under which rabbits live on many small islands all over the world. Moreover, we had brought the population to this high level by a gradual process over two or three years. We had not, as has been done in other experiments we read of, suddenly filled an enclosure with numbers of adults unable to find breeding or living territory in a small space. When Barnett (1958) introduced twenty-four 'interloper' rats into a small compound containing a colony of six brown rats, the resident rats, settled some time before and living harmoniously in their separate territories, attacked or menaced the interlopers. Unable to escape, the interlopers lay prostrate, breathing irregularly; six of them died on the first day, eleven on the second to seventh days, and five later; only two interlopers survived. Those which had died had little or no marks of violence – they had died of heart-failure following the sudden psychological 'insult'! Death from shock is known in many animals, from man to bird. We have taken up small wild birds, caught in outhouses or ringing traps, which have been in a coma of fright, prostrate, heart beating violently but otherwise unhurt, and some have never recovered; while others actually appear to feign death or coma, and will suddenly fly away, fully alert. The latter behaviour is akin to that of the rabbit and hare, which will often crouch perfectly still, as if in a trance, in order to escape the notice of a passerby; we have sometimes been able to pounce on and hold crouching rabbit or hare.

A simpler term for psychological or psycho-physiological or sociopsychological (three adjectives used by biologists) 'insult' might be simply 'chagrin' or a state of fret. We believe that some adult male rabbits in our enclosures may have died of sheer lack of will to live, once they had been dispossessed of mate and chivvied out of breeding territory by dominant males, and forced to live skulking lives in conditions of poor shelter and unpalatable food supply. It is known that blood-sugar levels fall during periods of malnutrition; and that if weakened animals are under further physical stress, as when pursued by enemies, they will sometimes collapse and die without being killed, like Barnett's rats. Rabbits pursued by stoat or weasel, muskrats pursued by mink, caribou by wolf, have been recorded as slowing down in their escape flight, then dragging their legs helplessly or standing still and showing symptoms of paralysis, which enables the pursuer to close upon the pursued almost at leisure. (But it is also a useful function of predators to kill off the weakling and diseased individuals of their prey, which, because of their weakness, are the first to succumb; this, of course, ensures the survival of the fittest.)

Recent example of a population crash on the severest scale occurred in the rabbit population of Skokholm, following the summer drought of 1959. Less than 150 out of the island's estimated total of 10,000 rabbits survived the succeeding winter. But as the island was unoccupied by observers in that winter the exact cause of the calamity, which was more violent than any recorded in the thirty-two years of documented rabbit-history of Skokholm is not known. It could not have been myxomatosis, for the reason given later in this book (page 122). It may have been coccidiosis induced indirectly by severe malnutrition.

Hugh Lloyd has told us what happened next, as fortunately he was at the time studying the island rabbits during the summer. Pasture did not recover until midsummer. It was then so plentiful that the adult does came back into oestrous condition in September and October (an unprecedented happening on Skokholm) and each had at least one litter then. In 1961 breeding continued on a high level of fertility; the food supply was abundant for the next two years of low population. In his studies of Skokholm rabbits in years of both minimum and maximum population, Lloyd finds that there is no observable intra-uterine mortality (resorption of embryos); he considers that the primary limitation of potential population increase on the island is achieved by the short breeding season, confined in normal conditions of over-grazed degenerate pasture (= food shortage) to about ten weeks' duration.

Conditions in the summer of 1960 on Skokholm were, in fact, close to those in the Extensive Enclosure C at Orielton, known as Savanna. Here in 1956, as at Skokholm in 1960, were but one or two rabbits to one acre of grazing. With more than enough food, and with no overcrowding, how do rabbits behave?

The events under these ideal conditions in Savanna are described in the next chapter.

8 The Idyll in Savanna

And O the spring – the spring!
I lead the life of a king!
Couched in the teeming grass,
I spy each pretty lass – KEATS

The one-acre Enclosure C was a lawn-like savanna of coarse grass typical of parkland which has lain unploughed but grazed and/or cut for hay for hundreds of years. The composition of the sward – largely wild plants in 1955 – is described on page 29. There were a few clumps of coarse weeds: nettles around the one tree, a great elm, and meadowsweet thick along the southern fence where the shade of the roadside trees kept the ground moist.

During the spring of 1955 we had not enough rabbits to spare to establish the nucleus in Savanna. As a result of no grazing a hay crop grew up and had to be cut and taken away in July. We introduced sheep at intervals to keep the grass short enough to clear observation of the rabbits; the sheep reduced coarse 'weeds' and improved the pasture to the benefit of the rabbits in succeeding years.

As soon as the hay was cleared we introduced a male rabbit brought to me by a farm worker who had caught it in the woods. It was then (July 31st) not quite full-grown, about eight months old. The testes were invisible as yet.

There were no natural burrows in Savanna. Lone Buck lay out in the longer tufts of grass left from the hay cutting. From the tree-hide we noted that he frequently visited the wire netting wall separating Savanna from Plain, and ran up and down there, looking for a place to break through and join the Plain rabbits.

He was not lonely for long. We took a young doe from Plain, about sixteen weeks old, and placed her in Savanna. As there were no natural burrows we dug out a spit of ground about four feet by six feet and one foot deep and placed four rusted discarded 10-gallon milk churns on their side, two facing east, two facing west. We heaped the displaced earth above and around them, and scattered dry soil inside them to give the occupants a level warm floor.

For no special reason we called this young doe Sheba, and placed her in this Palace of the Churns. This artificial home was dry but perhaps too airy and cold. Perhaps there was too much condensation on the metal walls and roof? Perhaps its structure – four cylindrical recesses and no bolt-holes or escape exits but only the one aperture to each churn – was unacceptable, for rabbits like to have a second exit. She never accepted it save as a rare refuge when hunted by us during a subsequent round-up, or when driven from a natural burrow which she proceeded to dig at intervals during that winter.

Sheba was born too late to breed before the spring of 1956. Lone Buck chased her, licked her face and loved her through the winter; and in April the first babies appeared – four of them in the nursery stop E which she had dug far to the east of the Palace of the Churns, almost as far as she could go from the busy warrens of Plain (Fig 1).

This was a little awkward for the observers on the Tree Hide. Sheba lived a little too far for us to catch the smaller details of her behaviour through binoculars. We had to use the big telescope on her. However, as she was the sole mature doe in Savanna it was easy to follow her main movements – when she made any.

Sheba was not one for movement. She stayed around her nursery, the picture of self-satisfaction, of wife-mother, contented in undisputed possession of home and unlimited food supply. In four months, April to July, she produced regularly her litters at E; this indicated that she had mated and conceived on or about the second day following each of the first three parturitions.

As soon as we could we tried to catch up and remove from Savanna all her weanlings, if possible before the weanlings of the next litter appeared. Often there was natural predation to help us. The buzzards would sit in the great elm on a fine afternoon, waiting for the kittens to appear. There would be a noiseless glide, a squeal if the pounce was successful; and the little rabbit would be dead in a few seconds – the death grip of this predator is an inter-locking device of eight long rapier talons entering its victim's body. Gone-wild cats also stalked and carried off some of the inexperienced weanling rabbits.

We removed twelve of Sheba's young ones in 1956, possibly just over half of the total born. One young doe escaped our attempts to round her up and also the attention of the buzzards and cats. We decided to let this daughter of Lone King and Sheba remain. She was christened Miriam and became very friendly with her father. That is to say she spent much of her adolescence with him in his incessant patrol of the boundary fence. She gazed with him upon the events of the crowded community of Plain. They sat together, at times side by side, like parent and child gazing at the crowded inmates of the monkey pen at the zoo. It was as fascinating to Miriam and Lone King as it was to the human observers. Both exiled rabbits longed, it would seem, to explore the city of Plain.

Lone King remained undisputed king by this artificial removal of all his children save one daughter. Of course he easily 'dominated' the two females, his queen and daughter. But it was not real dominance. He merely possessed the two does in the absence of any effective male opposition. In fact, they dominated him subtly, as wives dominate husbands, by allowing him the freedom of pursuing them when they were in a mood to be pursued, a mood of play, of libido; but if they were in no mood for play or love they would turn on him, box their paws in the air as a warning for him to keep away. This signal seemed to inhibit his desire to follow them, and he desisted.

Lone King yielded to us useful information on the natural behaviour of the male rabbit with plenty of living space. From the moment of his introduction as an adolescent buck in the, to him, almost boundless Savanna, he sought to get close to the nearest rabbit community. This was an exhibition of the gregarious nature of his species or at least his sex of the species; and Miriam had shown that the young female was also gregarious.

It seemed obvious to us that Lone King would never be satisfied until he could actually enter the populated warren of Plain, and establish himself in whatever niche, whatever position in the hierarchy, he could secure by his own strength and experience or skill. We do not believe he was conscious of this need on those terms; he did not say to himself: 'That big buck in Plain is always displaying at me, and I at him. I could easily beat or kill him and win my way to the king position in that great palace of ANE.'

From our limited knowledge of rabbit intelligence, acquired by observation, we believe he was impelled to run up and down the wire-netting division because he could see other rabbits moving around, and was intensely stimulated, from the inherent gregariousness of his species, to join more closely in their social activities. The wire-netting division frustrated him, prevented the fighting which would decide his position in this society to which he belonged by right of his natural sociality.

Lone King was ready to attack any other bucks, especially those which came close to the netting and displayed at him, and they in their turn were prepared to attack him as a potential trespasser (albeit inaccessible), at the enforced impassable artificial boundary created by the millimetre-thick wire-netting. And Lone King did try to attack them as soon as his libido increased with the development of his testes. He began to display more often, in September and October; he acquired the habit of leaping at any buck which came up close to the netting; leaping at, and even insulting them.

The log-book, for instance, records that on October 10th Lone King urinated during a leap at the young buck Daredevil who was sitting quietly by the fence. Evidently the urine was squirted with accuracy, since Daredevil hastily retired about three yards from the fence, and proceeded to shake his ears, and to wash his face, ears and his body fur thoroughly.

Sometimes Lone King scratched holes at the base of the netting, trying to get through. We filled in these scrapes each day on our morning inspection round. They would doubtless, if left, have resulted in a communicating passage – except that the buried (reversed T) netting would have baffled the rabbit. But Lone King never worked at a scrape for long, just a few seconds at a time; it was really a form of displacement activity, releasing the tension built up in his failure to get to grips with the rabbits beyond the fence. Sometimes this tension was expressed in furious biting at roots, even at the netting, exposed in the shallow excavation of the 'scrape'.

In his three breeding seasons in Savanna Lone King spent his time, during most of the hours we observed him in dawn and evening watches, patrolling along the boundary with Plain. He wore a path there with his incessant padding. This was the artificially enforced limit of his territory, the line which he defended entirely by vigorous display – since fighting was impossible. That track, that footpath, that artificial demarcation line became not only worn almost bare; it was heavily impregnated with the insignia of the rabbit. It was marked visibly with Lone King's faecal pellets. It was marked invisibly, but none the less effectually, with the olfactory badge of the king buck; with urine, and with scent droplets from the chin of Lone King which developed quite a matted beard by his second spring. A healthy master buck of Savanna was Lone King, his virile personality preserved by the constant exercise of display without the dangers of fighting, by unlimited food supply, and by the consummation of his libido upon wife and daughter.

Lone King illustrated what life could be like in complete freedom, in a wild state, where the rabbit population is as low as one pair to the acre – a density probably much in excess of average population figures for rabbit-inhabited country in the United Kingdom. And although his children in the enclosure were not secure from avian and feline predators, he himself was powerful enough to be safe from all enemies save man, disease and senility.

We take leave of Lone King, basking in the comparative freedom we had given him in Savanna, yet not consciously aware of his good fortune; and – such is the ambition of the male animal – at intervals frustrated by the enticements of inaccessible neighbours and territory in the midst of the happiness of family life (which he so visibly enjoyed) and sound health.

We turn to his mate Sheba, to follow the life of a doe in the same comparative freedom. Here is a very different picture.

Sheba, sensible woman, had no lasting ambition, it seems, to return to the turmoil of the city of Plain. After we introduced her to Savanna and her future mate in the autumn of 1955, Sheba quickly adjusted to the new freedom of one acre of grazing much richer than that of Plain. As she had been late born in Plain and was therefore one of the lowest ranking in the hierarchy there she exhibited at first the usual timidity of a person of inferior status. She ran from every other rabbit, including Lone King.

Sheba explored timidly on her first evening when she emerged from the Palace of the Churns which we had provided for her. It had been a terrifying experience to be chased and captured one dewy morning, and held, kicking wildly, in a vice-like grip by man; then ear-tattooed and ear-tagged; and then popped into an unfamiliar vault-like barrel of metal with an earth floor and a ray of light to indicate the only exit to the boundless plain of Savanna. No wonder she got away as soon as possible, and hopped uncertainly, miserable and lost, sniffing the air hopefully for familiar scents, back towards Plain.

At the dividing fence, she encountered Lone King. He ran towards her. She fled along his fence-side path, and as he followed, she doubled back, running to and fro for a few seconds, dodging him. Becoming more excited, as if he had suddenly realised for the first time that a rabbit was really on his side of the fence, and accessible at last, he darted upon her. She bounced against the netting in a vain attempt to return home to Plain, and to escape the buck.

Suddenly she seemed to realise that a vast country lay open behind her; and she escaped – inferior as she was – racing away to the east, covering some fifty yards non-stop across the enclosure. She circled the elm tree and crouched down, practically invisible in the cover of long withered grass.

Lone King followed; but presently returned, alone, to his stamping ground along the fence. Darkness fell. We abandoned our watch.

Sheba did not return to the Palace of the Churns, and its terrifying association with the human hand. She resumed the habits of adolescence. Since she had left the nursery where she had been born in Plain she had lived out in the open air in a squat or form (from which we had surprised her on the day of her capture). She slept out in the same way in Savanna; that is to say, she rested and dozed by day in a squat, warmed by the sun, cooled by the wind and rain, all through the autumn.

Lone King did not care for the Palace of the Churns either; this was perhaps because Sheba had disdained out of fear this unsuitable man-made dwelling. It was obvious in our studies that the buck depended on his doe to choose the home, to decide where to live. And thus Lone King ignored the dry shelter of the Palace and slept out alongside Sheba – as soon as she had become psychologically adjusted to him. It took several days for her to accept his presence even near to her. The barrier of fear which the pressures of population in Plain had engendered in Sheba from the moment of being bullied by older more powerful neighbours was not, in fact, broken down for several weeks. The buck's approaches terrified her. She kept the rule of individual distance learned from the bitter discipline of life in Plain; she moved so that at least one yard separated her from Lone King. It was some weeks before she seemed to recognise that his advances were amatory, not bellicose. She was still very young, virgin, and not desirous of a mate.

She began to frequent a small, low anthill close to the eastern boundary of Savanna, far from the sight of the events in Plain. We saw little of Sheba at this distance. She remained most of the hours of daylight in one of several squats she had made with the impression of her body – hunched in the dead grass. Here Lone King would visit her, but soon he would abandon her in order to resume his late afternoon, evening and dawn patrol along the boundary with Plain.

The leaves had fallen. November, dull days, rain; and little direct observation possible.

Winter had come. Fur lay around in the dew of Plain and Wood. The rabbits were fighting, mating. There was no fur visible in Savanna. Lone King did not have to fight in order to mate with Sheba.

Our morning stroll around the enclosures proved that Sheba was digging her own warren into the dry base of the little anthill far away at E.

Here she made her first nursery. Out of the earth here appeared her first children, four kittens which attracted our attention one April afternoon.

A buzzard sat in the great elm close by, silent and ready.

Heavy rain in May 1956 flooded the nursery at intervals. One morning a kitten of the second litter was found freshly dead at the entrance, as if pulled forth by Sheba; it had disappeared by the evening, no doubt carried off by the buzzard, which does not disdain carrion.

It was clear to us that Anthill Warren E had been dug in a poor situation. Sheba had been induced to make a home there by finding the tiny dry anthill, a landmark which, apart from the rejected Palace of the Churns, was the highest and driest portion of the level grassland of Savanna. Before it had been enclosed Savanna, in fact, had never attracted a wild population to settle on its smooth surface, so liable to filling and flooding in heavy rains. As we were responsible for keeping the rabbits prisoner there we began to realise that we must help them to help themselves to live more comfortably in drier quarters, if they were to remain healthy and breed successfully.

We dug a trench a few yards from the Palace of the Churns and threw up a bank of soil, adding to this until it was three feet high and well stamped down, and covering some six feet square. We capped this with the turf cut from the site and poked a few exploratory holes at ground level as an invitation to burrow. This site, convenient for observation from the Tree Hide, was in the north-west corner and therefore received the label of CNW. It was complete by June 3rd 1956.

Rabbits are essentially suspicious of man's activity. Sheba did not accept this gift of a dry mound until weeks and months had passed. Without Sheba's approval it was of course not acceptable to Lone King. And as we have said, we have never seen a buck excavate a home – this is the woman's job.

Lone King, however, inspected it on the eighth evening, scratched perfunctorily around on the top, chinned the drying turf with his scent droplets, and deposited faecal pellets. It was thus marked out as a part of his territory.

No one disputed this claim. There was none to dispute it. No rabbits were interested in CNW for a long time. Sheba continued to enlarge Anthill E, where she brought up her fourth brood early in July. For a while she enjoyed (if such is the correct interpretation, as we believe it is) life as a mother with her weanlings there, until we removed them, leaving only the uncatchable Miriam.

Miriam, with that natural wanderlust or urge to emigrate which assails almost all adolescent animals, from intelligent man to unintelligent bird and insect, wandered restlessly about the enclosure of Savanna in the lovely summer afternoons, sometimes playing games with her younger brothers and sisters (for as long as they were there), sometimes hopping about among grazing sheep (when these were at intervals present) with friendly curiosity, often sitting beside her father on watch at the fence, and gazing upon the activities of the other rabbits in Plain.

Miriam began to frequent the fine dry hillock thrown up at CNW. She was joined by some of the kittens wandering from Anthill E: but we soon took them away from her. Lone King was her sole playmate. He exhibited towards her all the tenderness of a loving father. They chased each other and frisked around the dry heap. They rested together side by side. He licked her. She licked him – a pretty sight, the little daughter and the big, tough-looking father.

Miriam began to dig into the base of the dry mass of CNW and open up a home of her own. Lone King did not bother to help her.

This was the autumn of 1956. The queen Sheba remained at her Anthill Burrow E. She had poor if sufficient quarters, though damp and frequently flooded in the winter. She had no one to trouble her except Lone King, who attended to her sexual satisfaction at appropriate intervals as soon as he was fertile and potent that autumn. Young, ripening daughter Miriam was no trouble to Sheba at first. We believe that they all slept together in the autumn, before the burrows dug in CNW were big enough to house a rabbit, although we cannot prove this; we base this belief on parallel events observed in the artificial underground warren D. The trio were a happy family.

Miriam was old enough to conceive at the turn of the year. Doubtless this development had triggered off in her the desire to dig deeper into the comfortable dry mound of CNW. She hid her first litter here in January 1957 while continuing to visit the queen's house at E.

But when her weanlings burst out of the sides of CNW Miriam remained with them, guarding them, enjoying her maternity. Why move? It was a much more comfortable dwelling-place than the miserable, often flooded Anthill Burrow E.

Sheba may have thought so, too. But how can we tell what Sheba thought? She was queen of Savanna by right of seniority, of experience and of physical strength, a young wife entering her second season of kitten production. We do not know what went on in her brain; but we can imagine what was troubling her in the spring of 1957, what caused her to act as she did in a way not usual for an established queen.

Sheba had worked hard at the Anthill site. By January 1957 it was enlarged with three entrances/exits. One of these exits sloped away on the lower side of the anthill warren and drained the upper portion of the warren to some extent, so that it was not completely waterlogged in the rains.

Once more Sheba deposited her first litter there, in December. Heavy rains flooded and drowned the kittens in January 1957. We found one, about ten days old, floating in the mouth of the lower exit.

Sheba moved over to CNW, defeated by weather, abandoning the home she had laboriously made for herself and held so tenaciously over five full-term pregnancies and lactations.

How did Miriam welcome her mother's appearance in CNW? Did she, as sole occupant of the new warren, drive Sheba away? Did she welcome her mother as someone she knew well, a friend, even perhaps with true filial humility?

We shall never know, not the exact details. All we were able to record was the sudden presence of Sheba with her daughter at CNW, both busy, digging new holes, breeding and rearing families in the dry mound, which increasingly became a labyrinth of passages, entrances and exits.

No dissension was recorded between the two breeding does at CNW. Admittedly they did not sit touching each other, side by side, but nor did they fight. They were tranquil, each busy about her own affairs of feeding and breeding. CNW had become the royal residence where Queen Sheba retained her queenship, or at least went unchallenged as queen by her daughter, Miriam. The wet Anthill Burrow E was neglected, as unvisited as the rusting Palace of the Churns. Only Lone King made a visit now and then to the tops of Anthill and Churns and there renewed the royal insignia of his office, as master of Savanna – a few pellets, a little urine perhaps and a droplet of male scent from his encrusted chin – a gesture, in this case (as none challenged him) signifying nothing effective.

There was room for two queens in Savanna; they need never trouble each other with jealousy in matters of sex, Lone King supplied all requirements there; as for nesting territory, CNW was large enough for two does not to be in each other's way in the dry (and so comfortable) interior; and the same went for grazing competition, so abundant was the grass, and of such fine quality.

The two mothers were not even troubled with problems of keeping their children in order. The little ones were removed before they became a nuisance and got on parental nerves.

Is it surprising that the three adults – king, queen and princess – stuck together so amicably? Picture to yourself the situation of living on an island with abundant food and ideal housing conditions, and a splendid area for exercise but no possibility of escaping to join the world of mankind. You (man, wife and daughter) are able to breed, but all your children mysteriously disappear. There is no problem of having to divide up the island territorially, between sons and daughters desiring living space and prepared to fight you for it. You can see all that, strife and distress included, in progress on the next island. But it doesn't touch you. You are free, and yet a prisoner.

Under these circumstances wouldn't you stick together, be friendly, be loving, be anxious to have children, to try and keep things going into your old age, to huddle together against the huge, enveloping, perhaps menacing loneliness in the midst of plenty?

Wouldn't you, wouldn't you . . .?

Did these three adults think of their predicament? Were they puzzled at all? Was their philoprogenitiveness affronted by the Pied Piperesque disappearance of their progeny? Was their natural gregariousness unsatisfied? Or were they as ignorant and happy as they were robust and healthy?

On the surface, to the human observer, life in Savanna seemed idyllic – for a grown-up rabbit.

9 Life Underground

A bower quiet for us, and a sleep
Full of sweet dreams, and health, and quiet breathing – KEATS

The artificial warren, known as The Underground, or more briefly as 'D', described earlier (page 31), was designed to enable us to study the individual rabbit in its burrow, under conditions of closely controlled habitat and pasture.

In Chapter 4 we have described the battle in Plain between rival kings Big Boss and Bold Benjamin induced by our artificial removal to Wood and return to Plain three weeks later of Big Boss. He was a mainland-born buck, heavier by half a kilogram than Benjamin. But he was suffering from a fear psychosis, due to his sojourn in a new hostile territory from which he could not escape, at the moment when he was suddenly returned to his home environment. His successor there had meanwhile become dominant buck; in the exuberance of that dominance Benjamin attacked and defeated the exiled king.

We have related how the ex-king gradually recovered some of his former dominance by acquiring territory in one corner of Plain. He re-established himself at ANE in Plain in the autumn. We had, however, decided to remove both these dominants in order to record the struggle for dominance in the young secondary bucks. We opened up the burrows in July 1956 and removed Boss from the royal palace at ANE and Benjamin from his 1955 home at ASW.

It was the neutral season. Bucks no longer fought. Their testes had shrunk or ascended into the abdomen, leaving the scrotum flaccid and empty. This was a favourable period to commence our study of behaviour below ground.

We placed one buck in each of the two separate artificial passages leading to the two interior chambers communicating against the plate glass, on July 21st 1956 (Plate 5). A young doe, Dorothea, was also released in the enclosure and left to choose her home on her own account.

We allowed them to settle down, unvisited, for five days. There was no sign of fighting. By the third day it was seen that all three were feeding normally at the same time in the late afternoon as the inmates of the adjoining Wood and Plain. And they were already becoming indifferent to a red electric light we left burning inside the observation hut.

On the fifth day we kept a twenty-four-hour watch on The Underground, three of us taking turns to sit in the shelter of the hut and record every observed movement of the three rabbits.

It was interesting to find that during the day the two kings were sitting side by side in the cellar, while the young doe was resting alone in the passage above at S. This friendliness confirmed that, in the neutral season, like the stags of the red deer herd in the off season, male rabbits are able to live close together amicably. Although deadly rivals in the rutting period, they got together during the hours of rest below ground, once more demonstrating to us their gregarious, even sociable, habits.

Sociability is valuable, even essential, in a species that retreats for safety into confined quarters below ground. A daily check-up on their positions each morning, and occasional watches of from two to twenty-four hours, gave us a clear picture of the behaviour pattern of the rabbit under ground. So long as the neutral season lasted, July to October inclusive, the two adult bucks usually remained together in the Cellar of the Underground, and often Dorothea joined them. All three preferred to rest in the Cellar which was roomy, farthest from the entrances, and free of draughts. Over four years of observation of behaviour in this Underground Warren the sociable nature of the rabbit was many times demonstrated.

In January the adult bucks separated. The old king Big Boss retained the use of the Cellar where he sat with Dorothea, when she was at home. But during much of the spring days young Dorothea preferred to sit in the narrow gangway at the S. entrance. Benjamin rested in the long passage against the glass between S. and N. exits. This was the renewal of territoriality, with the onset of libido or breeding. As already demonstrated in earlier chapters, during the breeding season buck rabbits establish definitive and strongly defended territories and these territories are so sharply defined that, according to W. E. Poole, they will not leave them even when lured by attractive food bait placed outside.

Fighting began in January; that is, we found fur lying about the grazing area of the Underground Pen. As it was not natural for two mature bucks to be confined in such close grazing quarters we removed Big Boss altogether. His usefulness was at an end, and he was painlessly killed. As a mainland-born buck he had always been a little out of place among the other island-born rabbits.

Old Benjamin and young Dorothea settled down to breed in The Underground. For a nursery we had provided a special chamber, with a separate entrance (see Plate 5) for Dorothea, covering the glass there with a sheet of cardboard so as to give privacy, and putting down a bed of earth and a little dried grass to encourage her to make her nest close to the glass so that we could study maternal behaviour.

However, she did not accept this blandishment. She inspected the Nursery, to our knowledge, only once. She preferred to dig her own nesting stop in the open compound. Here she raised two broods to weaning age. Almost before most of these were weaned, as they began to run about the entrance to the nesting stop, local gone-wild and domestic cats studied and stalked them. It was too easy for cats to capture the weanlings in the confined space of this small grazing enclosure. Our placing the weanlings in the concrete passages did not help; they ran back to the natural nesting burrow in which they had been born. But three kittens survived the visits of the cats and were half-grown by mid-July when the doe ceased to produce live young. We blocked up this outdoor nesting stop to prevent its development into a burrow.

The young rabbits were by this manœuvre driven to join their parents in the concrete warren. We could observe behaviour of the family underground.

The buck and doe usually rested in the deepest part of the artificial warren, in the Cellar. They cuddled close together, sleeping, dozing, preening, occasionally eating (reingesting) the cud, that is, collecting a pellet from the anus, and swallowing it. They were otherwise inactive all through the summer day from about sunrise to mid-afternoon.

The youngsters were a little more active, and after resting all morning they became restless after midday. They hopped along the burrow passages against the glass, and explored the tunnel exits. But they returned time and again to their mother, pushing their way between her legs. At intervals they sucked milk. Early in July, when she ceased breeding, it seemed clear that she had some milk left, because she tolerated a longer period of dragging at her teats by the babies of her final litter now that she was no longer pregnant.

The buck took no notice of his children underground. He was, however, not hostile. When they pushed between him and the doe, and snuggled together, with mother on one side and father on the other, he made no effort to displace them. He seemed rather to enjoy the warmth of their bodies close against his (Plate 6).

It was a pleasant domestic scene. The heads of the kittens would gradually droop lower and lower as they dozed; now and then they would be jerked upright, only to fall again in sleep. The adults might also doze, but usually their heads were hunched back on the shoulders when the eyes were closed. They appeared to rest and doze like this without losing consciousness. The buck appeared more awake than the doe, more as it were on guard. But there was no protective significance in their respective positions: the buck was sometimes on the outside of his mate and children, and sometimes on the inner side away from the approach passage. Their relative positions obviously depended on which individual entered the burrow first.

From many hours of watching the behaviour of the adults and the young in the artificial warren, it was clear that the rabbits enjoyed a family life below ground. Buck and doe accepted their progeny in the home for long after weaning time, and all through the neutral season – July to October – the growing youngsters might sleep by day in contact with the adults.

Their behaviour in these artificial conditions underground, to which they had become accustomed, was so natural and easy that it would be fair to assume that this behaviour was typical of what went on in the darkness of natural burrows. Certainly the outward evidence of this behaviour exhibited by the presence of mated pairs and their young sitting amicably side by side at the entrance to natural burrows in Plain and Wood confirms our belief in family togetherness in the rabbits.

We have already said that sociability (which one dictionary defines as 'the practice of family intercourse') must be important and have survival value in a gregarious species, living much of its life in confined, underground quarters. And from the behaviour of the two ex-king bucks, neutral in the neutral season, and separated but living in the same burrow system in the breeding season, we may suppose that as long as the dominant buck had the best quarters, the secondary buck would be allowed to live in the secondary quarters of the same warren. That was the degree of sociality, close in the neutral season, guarded in the breeding season.

It was clear, too, from the observations quoted in this and previous chapters, that the children of the king and queen, living in the best quarters, and having the best grazing areas defended and kept for themselves by the dominance of the king, would have these advantages over the children of the secondary pairs: better accommodation, better food, and better protection at least during childhood and adolescence. They would therefore be better-grown, stronger, more dominant individuals than those born outside the royal quarters.

10 Reingestion

Whatsoever parteth the hoof and is cloven-footed and cheweth the cud, that shall ye eat. Nevertheless these shall ye not eat of them that chew the cud – the coney, because he cheweth the cud, but divideth not the hoof; he is unclean to you –

AUTHORISED VERSION

The rabbits did nothing much underground. They rested. They slept for hours. Being clean animals they preened (much as a cat does, with tongue and forepaws) every part of the fur of the body.

Rabbits spend about half their life underground (if we average their winter and summer hours of grazing above and of resting below ground). It is essential to the health of a numerous burrowing animal to keep at least the sleeping quarters clean. But rabbits go further – they do not even use latrines underground, as do rats and lemmings (the latter living under the snow in winter). They eat their own excrement; and we never observed them to pass urine in the artificial burrow.

Life underground was for the rabbit, perhaps, close to the poets' pleasant sleep in which sweet dreams drifted by. So peaceful was it that our several twenty-four-hour watches at the artificial burrow were at times boring – this incessant dozing and sleeping and inactivity of the rabbits was even infectious. It lasted from the moment they returned from grazing in early morning until late afternoon when grazing was resumed. Our watches overnight were almost totally unproductive, except as to negative evidence. The rabbits remained grazing out of doors all night. On rare occasions one might return below for an odd minute, even an hour, to rest and preen, and reingest.

However, so long as we could watch the rabbits underground we had an ideal opportunity to study the phenomena of coprophagy or reingestion.

The fact that rabbits (the Bible rabbit, strictly speaking, is the related hyrax) and hares 'chew the cud' was recorded in the Bible. It is mentioned in *Leviticus*, Chapter 11, as written under the title of this chapter. Also (the

Jewish law of clean and unclean meats) in *Deuteronomy* XIV: 'Thou shalt not eat any abominable thing. These are the beasts which ye shall eat: the ox, the sheep, and the goat, the hart and the roebuck, and the fallow and deer, and the wild goat, and the pygarg, and the wild ox, and the chamois. And every beast that parteth the hoof, and cleaveth the cleft into two claws, and cheweth the cud among the beasts that he shall eat. Nevertheless these ye shall not eat of them that chew the cud, or of them that divide the cloven hoof; as the camel, and the hare, and the coney: for they chew the cud, but divide not the hoof; therefore they are unclean unto you.'

Later writers, even authorities on both wild and domestic rabbits, have seldom referred to this phenomenon. In general, textbooks on rabbit physiology and management ignore the subject, not because of its lowly theme but because the authors apparently were ignorant of it. Since its recent rediscovery it has been called 'reingestion', a suitable term implying that it is a form of re-eating and redigestion of food.

Certain grazing animals, such as cattle, goats, sheep, camel, giraffe and deer, regurgitate their food by passing up from the rumen balls of partly digested vegetable matter which is then masticated and ground up by the strong molar teeth before being swallowed once more. The remarkable process is best seen in the giraffe at the zoo; the progress of the ball of cud can be followed as, by a muscular action, it travels in the form of a substantial bulge up the long neck, to be trapped by the back teeth and ground into small fragments which, mixed with saliva, trickle back down the gullet without any obvious bulging of the neck. The complicated muscular processes involved include the retention within the stomach of the reingested matter at the same time as a fresh ball of cud is passed up to the mouth.

Not all grazing animals chew the cud or reingest. For example, the horse and swine families do not; we do not offer any explanation why, except to observe that both spend much of their time eating in order to sustain life, ingest large quantities of food and pass massive quantities of loose-textured dung. This suggests that their conversion of food into nutriment may be inefficient.

Many animals, including insects as well as hares and rabbits, have this habit of refection or reingestion. Thus termites may refect food as much as six times. The habit of reingestion would appear to be useful in those grazing animals which, like some deer, rabbits and hares, and insects, lie up in cover for long periods. With stomachs filled from rapid and heavy grazing for short periods, they can ruminate or reingest food at leisure and derive the fullest nutriment therefrom, while sheltering from enemies and weather.

This is particularly appropriate in the rabbit. We observed that when the wild rabbit first goes forth to graze in the late afternoon it eats voraciously, nibbling down grass and vegetation in scythe-like movements of the jaws from one side to another, raising the head at intervals to look around and perhaps to draw into the mouth, by a chewing action, any longer stalks of vegetation.

Perhaps after half an hour of grazing a rabbit will eat less indiscriminately, will cast about for plants which it finds more palatable. During this first hour, as the new green food accumulates in the stomach, the rabbit voids numbers of hard faecal pellets, probably as a result of the exercise as well as the increasing pressure of ingested food upon the intestines. (On an average an adult rabbit will evacuate 360 hard pellets – total weight about four ounces – above ground each twenty-four hours.)

The edge taken off its appetite the rabbit finds time to play, to explore, to bask in the sun, to make love, to threaten in display according to the hour and season. It returns to graze at intervals. It invariably preens its fur early in the proceedings; no doubt its ears and fur have picked up dust and particles of earth from the roof of the underground burrow where it had rested by day.

Reingestion or eating of excrement (faecal pellets) was seen occasionally out of doors. It could easily be overlooked by the casual observer. A swift bending of the head during which the long ears almost touched the ground between the hind legs, then the rabbit's head would come up and the jaws work for a few seconds as the pellet was swallowed and the tongue licked around inside the closed mouth afterwards. In the rabbit there is a curious infolding of the lower lips over the space between the incisor and molar teeth which protects and hides the tongue. The observer could not see the faeces because of the masking action and the closed mouth.

Reingestion was observed both out of doors by day and below ground; but was most easily studied through the window of the artificial burrow. Here it was most frequent between 0800 hours and 1700 hours GMT; that is, for ten hours or so after the night grazing period. However, it is an intermittent not an incessant action. For example, in a twenty-four-hour watch underground, three rabbits reingested a mouthful of pellets, respectively, on 37, 18 and 16 occasions.

It was interesting to find that, over four years of observation in the artificial warren, we did not once record a rabbit deposit pellets or urine in the concrete-walled earth-carpeted burrows. Occasionally, in wet weather, a pellet might be brought below, stuck to the foot of a rabbit, and be shaken or preened off within. In that case the rabbit did not eat the pellet (which was generally squashed) and it remained on the floor of the warren and was trampled into the thin layer of earth we had originally scattered over the concrete floor.

Not only did each rabbit confine the deposit of excrement to the land outside, but it appeared to be able to produce only soft pellets while below ground and hard pellets in the open. How is this accomplished?

It is necessary to define the terms, soft pellet and hard pellet. If a rabbit is killed early in the evening and its viscera examined, the stomach will be found to contain a cluster of small, soft, dark, membrane-covered pellets (at one time these were erroneously thought to be made into this shape in the mouth); and the lower intestine leading to the anus will usually contain a string of large, hard and less viscid pellets without protecting envelope. The hard pellets are composed of hay-like fragments of plant cuticle and stalk. They are evacuated above ground. Soft pellets (it is commonly believed) may be voided at intervals out of doors but are usually, if not invariably, collected as they cling to the anus, which is slightly everted to project them by muscular action; and swallowed without falling to the ground.

Our observation of the rabbit below ground, reingesting these pellets, shows that the soft pellets are usually produced several hours after grazing, on a full stomach, long after the main mass of hard pellets has been evacuated in the open earlier in the evening.

Research on coprophagy in rabbits by Mervyn Griffiths and David Davies in Australia (1963) has shown that soft pellets begin to form posterior to the colon in the hind gut (Fig 13) soon after the main mass of hard pellets has been evacuated and the stomach is filling up with newly grazed food.

Earlier workers (Thacker and Brandt, 1955) considered that the high protein content of soft pellets (relative to that of hard pellets) was due to a protein-rich mucous secretion on to the newly formed pellets within the caecum or blind gut at the beginning of the large intestine. Griffiths and

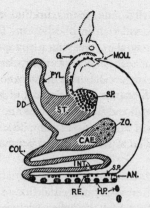

FIGURE 13. Simplified plan of viscera of rabbit to show reingestion process. AN – anus. CAE – caecum or blind gut. COL – colon. DD – duodenum. G – gullet or oesophagus. HP – hard pellets, evacuated. INT – intestine. MOU – mouth. PYL – pylorus. RE – rectum. SP – soft pellets, newly formed and swallowed in small clusters. ST – stomach full of vegetable matter newly ingested, with reservoir of reingested pellets which aid digestion. ZO – zone where soft pellets are first formed, partly from secretions of the caecum.

Davies have demonstrated that each soft pellet is separate and by the time it reaches the rectum is enveloped in a strong membrane. Its contents include much bacteria which account for the high proportion of protein. These soft pellets pass down to the rectum in glossy clusters. They are swallowed whole by the rabbit, that is, without breaking the enveloping membranes. This in itself is a remarkable feat, as, although the rabbit (under observation in the open as well as in our artificial burrow) sometimes appears to chew this faecal 'cud' after collecting it from the anus, with movements of the jaws varying in time from one to over one hundred seconds, Griffiths and Davies assert that the soft pellets are found whole in the stomach and therefore must be swallowed whole. The movement of the jaws may therefore be solely a swallowing, followed by a cleaning action of the tongue, during which saliva is ingested along with the soft pellets and must aid in the digestive process.

If a rabbit is put into a strait-jacket (experimenters have used a wide collar, also fitted leather 'pants') to prevent coprophagy, and if the soft faeces passed are placed in distilled water, each pellet in the cluster will imbibe water and separate and become spheres exactly as do those soft pellets which are reingested and found in the stomach normally. The membrane is quite tough and rich in phosphorus. If it is torn open with a needle the liquid contents flow out, leaving a collapsed envelope.

The fluid contents of the soft pellet from the rectum are revealed under a high-powered microscope as a rich flora of micro-organisms mingled with undigested cell walls of the plant food grazed by the rabbit. The nutrient bacteria are filamentous and rod-like, and there are cocci and cocco-bacilli. Parasitic oocysts and worm eggs can also be present. Griffiths and Davies were able to isolate typical lacto-bacilli from pellet material cultured in acetic acid broth.

These pellets on analysis contained (dryweight) about 56% bacteria. The protein content of the bacteria was 36%, and that of the plant matter 11%; or an average of 24.4% protein for the pellet, exclusive of the envelope. After being swallowed whole by the rabbit the soft pellets pass into the stomach where they do not immediately mingle with the normal contents of the stomach – the greenish chewed up plant material. These reingested pellets remain intact for up to six hours and as long as they remain intact the bacteria they contain remain viable, permitting active fermentation of carbohydrate to take place. They finally dissolve, yielding their concentration of phosphorus, sodium and potassium and lactic acid, to aid digestion and nutrition.

The process whereby the nutritious soft pellet, with its tough membrane, is reingested and remains for several hours to 'incubate' and produce lactic acid, is of course akin to the activity in the complicated rumen of sheep and cattle where freshly grazed food is attacked by micro-organisms and plant cellulose is broken down. And reingestion in the rabbit appears to be a useful, specific device, enabling it to remain underground for a long time without absolute hunger, and without soiling its burrow. Perhaps it has a further function in this respect – there have been numerous reports of rabbits, frightened by ferreting or trapping operations, or after heavy falls of snow, remaining below ground for days, even a week or ten days, without feeding and without soiling their burrows. These reports have not been fully documented, but if they are true it is possible that rabbits may reingest previously reingested food both in the form of soft and hard pellets many times over in emergency while unable to go forth to graze.

Dr C. R. Metcalfe of Kew examined hard pellets collected from the ground at Orielton, and reported that they consisted of plant remains, almost all of which he was able to identify by determination of characters of the epidermal cells through the microscope (a labour of love indeed!), including the fine hairs of stinging nettle *Urtica*, eaten by the hungry rabbit. The list of plants he compiled for us from this examination covered studies found in the enclosures. Thus, in developing detailed ecological studies, pellet analysis could prove a useful tool; rabbit pellets can provide valuable indices of the food plants eaten.

Before we finish with this lowly subject of ordure, perhaps we should note some observations we made on the number of pellets produced by the rabbit. We thought it might be useful to know this if one is trying to estimate the size of a rabbit colony in the wild from the number of pellets lying around the grazings and warrens. Professional rabbit-catchers do this, but in conversation with some of them we found their estimates were on the low side. They 'guessed' an output of about twenty to fifty pellets a day per rabbit. These figures had, of course, to be multiplied by the number of days during which a faecal pellet survived above ground – about one week in wet, and double that period in dry or frosty weather – before it disintegrated or disappeared. We were able to agree with this approximate 'decay rate' of a rabbit pellet; by tests we found that in mild, wet weather a pellet might vanish in two days, but usually three or four days, devoured by ground fauna (worms, slugs, beetles, flies), but in very dry, frosty weather a pellet could survive for three weeks, or even longer.

Observation of rabbits in the underground chamber (Pen D), proved that they never passed pellets there, as already mentioned. It was therefore easy to count all the excreted pellets, which lay on the grass out of doors, in the small grazing area of 250 square yards enclosed with netting. By removing and counting all the pellets every day for forty days, we could arrive at exact figures for the 'output' of a single adult buck living alone there (in D) over this period. During January the yield per day was lower than in April because, presumably, the buck ate less while the grass was not growing. On the first day of the experiment, January 16th, 1958, we collected 116 pellets, and on the last day, April 14th, 522 pellets: the average was 360 pellets per day. Full details have been published elsewhere (Lockley, 1962).

Owing to the variability of output according to season and appetite, it is virtually impossible to estimate a rabbit population with accuracy by counting only freshly dropped pellets (which are dark and viscid) over a representative section of a warren grazing area from which all pellets have been removed twenty-four hours previously – except under very favourable conditions. A movable frame was used by us, three feet by three feet (enclosing one square yard), and placed in forty-eight such cleared positions at random across a one-acre enclosure containing a known number of rabbits.

A simple formula is thus $\dfrac{A \times B}{C}$ where A = number of fresh pellets collected within 48 random square yards cleared 24 hours previously. B = 101, the nearest round number required to multiply 48 to 4,840 yards = 1 acre; C = 360, average output of faecal pellets per rabbit in 24 hours.

Thus the number of rabbits in this enclosed acre was

$$\frac{180 \times 101}{360} = 50.5$$

This formula proved approximately accurate in a test applied to the large population enclosed at Orielton, where pellets were uniformly dropped each day over a fairly uniform grazing surface. It would, of course, be very difficult to apply in estimating free wild populations in broken country and cover.

11 Population and Birth-control

Snowy flit of a scut,
He was in his hole:
And – stamp, stamp, stamp!
Through dim labyrinths clear;
The whole world darkened,
A Human near! – WALTER DE LA MARE

The rise and fall of rabbit empires, like those of man in history, and of lemmings in Scandinavia, is a phenomenon well known to man. Rabbits have become plagues in many places where they have been introduced, as in Australia and New Zealand. But in the land of their origin, the Mediterranean shores, they have long thriven in moderate numbers, often reduced or preserved by man, according to his whim or need. Here their populations have not fluctuated excessively; they are stable communities.

Rabbits have been introduced on small islands all over the world with varying success according to climate, and with most success on islands where the climate is temperate, neither too cold nor too hot, neither too wet nor too dry. In such situations, as on some islands off California, New Zealand, Australia, and many off the British Isles, they achieve, if left to themselves, maximum populations, according to food supply, of ten to fifty adults to the acre. Periodically, at peak heights of population, they are suddenly reduced, in a few months, to a fraction of these high numbers. As in our experimental pens, Plain and Wood, disease is induced by malnutrition and overcrowding.

We have described the spectacular decline in population known as a crash. Afterwards there is usually an abundance of food and territory as the over-grazed pasture recovers. The population feeds well and builds up rapidly for the next few breeding seasons. But it slows down as numbers approach 'capacity'.

While we were living on Skokholm Island over a period of twelve years the rabbit population was at first controlled by us. As described in the Introduction, we caught rabbits during our first two winters, and exported for sale

109

some two to three thousand, representing about a dozen rabbits killed from each of the 240 acres of grazing which the island afforded.

We have also noted (page 82) that only two types of rabbits were caught in winter on the island; a small thin rabbit born in the previous summer and a large fat rabbit above one year old. The young rabbit remained thin, and often very poor in condition until it had survived its first winter. It was the first to die in a crash. At one year old it began to fatten with the flush of grass in late April and May; we suspected – and H. G. Lloyd has confirmed – that the young doe would produce one small litter of two to four young only during this her first breeding season. She might produce two litters if feeding was exceptionally good and the spring season early; and she might do so also if the winter population had been low from a previous crash. But usually she produced one litter, often of only two live kittens.

After her second winter, the doe would produce two, sometimes three, litters between late March or early April and June. In July she ceased to breed. Her total annual production on this windswept over-grazed island was seldom more than eight live kittens in one season.

This low production is coupled with the poor physique of the island rabbit, which, as we have seen, weighs less and is smaller than the mainland of Britain rabbit. But after hundreds of years of conditioning to survive on impoverished grazing is the low production now a fixed ancestral pattern? Hugh Lloyd has shown (page 84) that it can change at once under conditions of plenty.

The production of wild does in New Zealand, where the climate resembles that of the rabbits' native Mediterranean, is often very high. Watson (1954) and others have shown that in areas where grazing is suitable and plentiful, old and dominant females may average over five young per litter and have five litters, that is up to twenty-seven kittens per female, but usually less, around twenty, in one season. The kittens of the first litter may breed in the same year; thus in a few spring and summer months a female rabbit can become a grandmother under the favourable New Zealand conditions.

Myers and Poole (1962), observing populations confined within two-acre enclosures in Australia, demonstrated that with increase in density, fecundity decreases. This confirms what happened in the stressed conditions in our Orielton one-acre enclosure. Myers and Poole reported that the decrease in fecundity, evidently due indirectly to tension and nervous stress occasioned by overcrowding and malnutrition, was the result of an increase in the rate of resorption of the young *in utero*, as well as of an apparent suppression of libido or oestrous behaviour.

These workers were able to show that in the Australian off season of dry hot weather there was no breeding and almost no social and territorial friction in the crowded colony. But as soon as the cool winter rains brought green pastures, reproductive behaviour became intense. As at Orielton, the size of territories held by bucks and their does decreased with population pressure, and fighting for the home ranges intensified.

When conditions were favourable, almost every litter born to each female after the first was conceived at the first 'heat' or oestrus (the post-partum oestrus) within twenty-four hours after parturition. As a result these does were pregnant almost continuously and dropped their litters at regular monthly intervals.

But in another year, with increased pressure of numbers, this periodic pattern of litter fall was interrupted, and although the does mated in the normal way at seven-day intervals (or multiples of seven days), there were fewer litters born live. Several live does examined (palpated) for pregnancy and found pregnant resorbed the embryos completely at about mid-term. Resorption, however, did not affect the seven-day (or multiple thereof) cycle of oestrous behaviour and mating.

The study by Myers and Poole confirms the classical work of Rogers Brambell in Wales (1944), who demonstrated the presence of a cycle in reproduction in females taken in the field by finding that does either carry their litters to full term or reabsorb the embryos between the eleventh and fifteenth day of gestation. Watson (1957) found another peak of resorption, about the twenty-first day, and Lloyd (1963) also found some pregnancies terminated about the sixteenth to twentieth day.

Brambell discovered that the rate of resorption in Wales was more or less constant throughout the breeding season, but Watson found variations according to the season in New Zealand, as did Mykytowycz (1960) and Poole (1960) in Australia.

Most workers agree in finding that in older, robust does resorption is less frequent than in young does in their first breeding season. Myers and Poole (1962) confirm that older does have larger and more frequent litters than young does. Older does are usually in the dominant positions in the hierarchy, but some are not and although it is not proved that rate of resorption is closely related to dominance, Mykytowycz states that the increase in resorption in overcrowded enclosure colonies was limited to subordinate does.

Resorption causes a remarkable physiological upheaval in the body, for it is an extremely rapid process. If it begins at half-term it can be over in two or three days, the embryos and embryonic and placental tissues shrivel and are resorbed into the maternal system. Milk appears in the mammary glands and the female comes in oestrus and mates as if parturition and birth of live young had occurred.

Brambell found that up to 60% of all litters conceived in does examined by him (1941-42) were lost by resorption. McIlwaine (1962) found that resorption of embryos occurred in 53% of 226 litters examined in New Zealand, and the greatest loss occurred in the first twenty days of pregnancy.

What is the significance of this high rate of resorption? Or indeed of high or low rates of resorption in the rabbit?

More work on the subject is necessary. But it is obvious that resorption is a form of natural birth-control in a potentially explosive breeder. At the time Brambell examined his 1,500 does, rabbits were abundant in the area in which these were killed. It may be that those pressures which limited the rate of increase in crowded enclosures (already described at Orielton and in Australia) were operating in the wild populations from which Brambell secured his specimens. Resorption is low and may be absent in females with abundant food and ideal conditions, as in our extensive enclosure Savanna.

Pre-natal mortality is part of the complex self-regulating fecundity mechanism of the rabbit. It can be triggered off by unfavourable conditions such as overcrowding (in enclosures and on islands) leading to psychological stress, and also apparently by deterioration of pasture, due to over-grazing or weather conditions. The actual physio-chemical process of resorption in the body is not understood, but is probably a function of the pituitary and other endocrine glands.

From a consideration of all the factors discussed above and in earlier chapters it is possible to postulate that the completion of pregnancy to full term (one month) with the fall of a normal-sized litter of four to five kittens only occurs when conditions of territory and food are satisfactory. Thus young does living in the subordinate positions, and less robust than older does,

frequently resorb part or all of their first litter, due possibly to these conditions plus a low body weight and lack of protein and other ingredients to
feed the developing embryos. These die, are reabsorbed, the doe's body
reserves are recruited thereby, she mates, and becomes pregnant again, this
time perhaps with better success if the external conditions are better as when
the spring flush of grass provides more nutritious food.

Resorption of embryos is less wasteful than abortion (premature birth),
which is difficult to detect and seldom recorded in the rabbit. Resorption is a
process, a form of birth control which helps to limit the population to the
food supply and territory available. It is not fully effective in this respect,
but it comes into play as a limiting factor before finally, if the population
continues to rise, disease causes a severe 'crash'.

An understanding of the chemical-physical process of the reaction which
starts off resorption is obviously important to man, whose numbers are rising
so rapidly. He may one day learn from a study of the rabbit, perhaps, how
to control his population problem by a resorption technique as well as by
the present use of oral and other contraceptive methods, and stop unwanted
human pregnancy early in the gestation period without the dangers and
unpleasantness of abortion. Man is rapidly approaching a state of overcrowding in his small world such as we have seen mirrored in the conditions
of rabbits confined on small islands. Territorial struggles (threats and little
wars) permit man and rabbit to maintain a place to live but only so long as
numbers are related to adequate food supply. When that relation is abused,
malnutrition and disease set in, as in the overcrowded regions of India and
China. But at present man continues to breed almost uncontrolled, and like
the rabbits is rapidly destroying his environment, by building over the face
of the land which is more than ever needed for the production of his food
and for his recreational needs. He is destroying his heritage; he is heading
for a crash, and this may be triggered off as in the rabbits by mechanisms
beyond his control, that is to say, beyond the control of the sane majority
of men. That trigger is likely to be a nuclear one, pulled by some dictator
or other madman whose endocrine glands, under territorial stress (fear
mania), like those of the rabbit in the same situation, are suddenly deranged
metabolically.

Man is unlike the rabbit in one respect; he does not live by bread alone.
But if he continues by over-population to burrow into and destroy the

countryside, killing out other forms of wild life, laying waste with bricks and concrete the few beautiful places on earth where he can rest and recuperate from the foul exhaust of his cities, he will indeed soon come to live by bread alone. Up to the time of the final crash he will live in a synthetic burrow, feed on frozen and tinned supermarket produce and pills, drink some of his own excrement (already today his excrement is discharged into rivers which are pumped into reservoirs to supply his medicated drinking water) and become as automated as, and even more helpless to avert disaster than, the rabbit.

12 Myxomatosis

Making everything afraid,
Wrinkling up his little face,
As he cries again for aid;
And I cannot find the place! – JAMES STEPHENS

In the autumn of 1953 the disease of myxomatosis appeared in rabbits in south-east England. It spread within a year over most of the British Isles, mowing down rabbit populations spectacularly. Farmers and foresters, whose crops and trees had suffered from over-population of rabbits, were suddenly relieved of an expensive pest, and were financially better off as a result of myxomatosis. But the appearance of the affected rabbits, with swollen heads, blind and deaf, and wandering helplessly along roads and fields, aroused a national indignation and outcry. 'Mercy squads' of men and women, chiefly from the towns, were set up by the Royal Society for the Prevention of Cruelty to Animals and other humanitarian organisations, to go forth and shoot or cudgel these dying rabbits to a more speedy death.

It is doubtful, however, if the myxomatous rabbit suffers as much as it appears to do or as much as the rat which dies a lingering death from phosphorus and other legalised rat-poisons; but then the poisoned rat usually dies unseen in its hole. Observations on myxomatous rabbits suggest that the swelling of the eyelids and ears which causes blindness and deafness also reduces sensitivity to pain, that it feels so little that its appetite remains unimpaired; and it is a fact that myxomatous rabbits will eat voraciously and even attempt to mate up to a few hours before death. Blindness, however, usually prevents their finding the path to the burrow and so they remain to die conspicuously in the open. The blind myxomatous rabbit is a pitiable object.

Myxomatosis was first described by Sanarelli in 1897; it had killed off most of his stock of European rabbits at the hospital in Montevideo. But it was not until 1942 that Aragão, after more than fifteen years of study, discovered that the myxoma virus, like influenza in man, occurred naturally but was comparatively benign or seldom fatal in the Brazilian rabbit *Sylvilagus brasiliensis*. Mosquitoes, or other winged vectors, biting the wild *Sylvilagus* rabbit in Brazil, and then attacking the domestic *Oryctolagus* European rabbit in hutches, conveyed the virus on their infected mouth-parts. The European rabbit, a recent importation to South America, had no resistance, and died easily, as the Eskimo and other isolated peoples are said to have done when they first encountered the virus of influenza introduced by white man.

The incubation period (i.e. the period between first infection and the appearance of symptoms) of the most lethal strain of the virus is about five days. The eyelids then begin to swell, and the inflammation quickly spreads to the base of the ears, the forehead and the nose; at the same time the anal and genital region becomes swollen. In the last stages the swellings discharge a serous fluid rich in virus material and the animal usually dies about the eleventh or twelfth day after it became infected.

Myxomatosis attacks no other animal fatally except the European rabbit; even hares are immune, except in a few very rare instances.

Aragão had already suggested in 1927 that myxomatosis might be the answer to the rabbit problem in Australia, where in 1887 the New South Wales authorities had offered £25,000 for a successful control technique. It was the Rabbit Destruction Committee of that State which provided the funds for the research carried out by Sir Charles Martin at Cambridge, England. The results of Sir Charles's experiments there were published in 1936. He showed that, using two strains of the myxoma virus obtained from South America, the weaker strain (A) killed off all but three of fifty-two tame rabbits and their progeny living in two enclosed colonies out of doors. The strain of higher virulence (B) exterminated two colonies of fifty-five and forty-four wild rabbits in the same enclosures. This was an encouraging start.

In 1936 Sir Charles approached me with the proposal that I allowed him to make a field test on a larger scale, for which he required a small island well isolated from the mainland. I was then living on Skokholm Island, Pembrokeshire, which carried at that time a dense population each autumn of up to 10,000 rabbits on its 240 acres. I agreed. I was very willing to abolish the uneconomic rabbits in order to obtain better grazing for our sheep flock.

In the autumn of 1936 Sir Charles stayed with us on Skokholm. Between us we caught, marked and inoculated eighty-three rabbits with strain B of the virus, and released them at points scattered over the whole island. Of these marked rabbits, twelve were found dead in the open during the next fortnight, after which the island was left unvisited for the winter. However, on returning to the island in the spring, we were disappointed to find no trace of myxomatosis in a population of rabbits which seemed as numerous as ever.

A second attempt was therefore made during the late spring of 1937, at a time when it was thought rabbits would be in closer contact during mating and breeding activities. Sir Charles was convinced that the virus was spread by direct contact, and that insect vectors were unimportant. Fifty-five rabbits were caught, marked, inoculated and released. For a while both marked and unmarked rabbits were found dead of the disease, but this soon died out with no obvious effect on the large numbers on the island.

A final attempt in the spring of 1938 was confined to inoculating seven rabbits from the same warren in the hope that a concentration of infected individuals might induce a local epidemic. But even this failed to kill all the members of the warren before it died out quickly.

This was a great disappointment to Sir Charles, and made his success with enclosed colonies at Cambridge inexplicable. The failure at Skokholm was not explained until twenty years later, when Sir Charles was on his death-bed.

The failure, however, had not deterred the Australian Government from encouraging further experiments, this time in Australia, where limited success was achieved in – as it proved later – unsuitable dry areas. In 1950 the virus was introduced into humid river areas and began to spread. It was found that in Australia certain mosquitoes were vectors; in swampy, warm conditions they acted as 'flying pins', conveying the virus from sick to healthy rabbits, on their mouth parts, without any development of the virus (as in malaria) within the body of the mosquito.

In three years of an intensive official campaign of aiding the natural spread by introducing the virus all over Australia, millions of rabbits were killed in areas where mosquitoes and rabbits coincided, chiefly in the south-eastern States. The dry areas were little affected. The campaign continues, as does the study of the virology of myxomatosis by Australian biologists. In

Australia the virus, although still effective, has become attenuated in local strains, and reduced from 99.8% mortality rate to 90% or less. The weaker strains of a virus take much longer to kill and thus an affected animal exists as a reservoir of infection for vectors for a correspondingly longer period; the attenuated strains have a selective advantage over the highly virulent strain in the process. In addition, the Australian rabbit is building up a degree of immunity to the disease which increases each year.

It is estimated that the increase of agricultural production since the success of myxomatosis in the south-eastern States of Australia has been worth some £50,000,000 annually.

This success in Australia encouraged the French scientist Dr Armand Delille, well-known for his work on the prevention of tuberculosis, and an entomologist of repute, to decide to introduce the virus in an attempt to destroy the plague of rabbits on his estate at Dreux, near Paris. He obtained some virus from a colleague at the Laboratoire de Bacteriologie, Lausanne, in June, 1952.

The full story of this introduction which caused the epidemic over the western countries of Europe, and the bitter controversy which accompanied it was told to us by Dr Delille's son when we visited the beautiful Chateau Maillebois (Eure-et-Loire) in December, 1953. At that moment Dr Delille was a very worried man; proceedings against him had been begun by the hunting and sporting interests in France, and he was engaged with his legal advisers in Paris preparing to defend his action in the law courts. A test case was being brought against him, with the financial backing of the hunting clubs of France, by a local owner of a domestic rabbitry in which the rabbits had all died of myxomatosis. Since the introduction of the disease in June, 1952, approximately 35% of the domestic and 45% of the wild rabbits in France had died of myxomatosis, according to the information supplied to us by the Pasteur Institute in Paris.

The Chateau Maillebois is a striking turreted medieval house lying in a beautiful wooded estate of 600 acres with a farm and small river, the whole enclosed with a high stone wall. This wall is broken only by certain entrance gates which had been rendered rabbit-proof before the introduction of the virus. Thousands of wild rabbits were devouring the farm crops and killing the tender forest trees, Dr Delille's son told us, when in June, 1952, two wild-caught rabbits were inoculated with the myxoma virus. In six weeks about 98% of the wild rabbits were dead, but none of the domestic rabbits in the hutches on the estate was affected.

In October, 1952, the disease was identified from a corpse picked up near Rambouillet, the residence of the President of France, fifty kilometres from Maillebois. According to Delille, the escape of the disease from Maillebois was artificial. Other landowners, learning of the success of the experiment, and refused permission to take diseased rabbits openly from Maillebois, broke into the estate by night and carried off sick rabbits. Delille believed that the mosquito was not a vector of the virus, because his own domestic rabbits had not been affected. However, it has since been proved that in the warm humid areas of France mosquitoes are carriers of the disease.

Dr Armand Delille did not announce his experiment until a year had elapsed and the disease was rampant in the majority of the Départements of France. On June 14th, and again on October 14th, 1953, he read papers to the Académie d'Agriculture, claiming great success for the method, and advocating the systematic use of myxomatosis for the control of rabbits. The admission raised a storm of controversy, in which the position of the Ministry of Agriculture in France was more equivocal than that of its counterpart in Britain. Responsible to the Ministry in France is the Conseil Supérieure de La Chasse, which derives its income from a levy on sportsmen in the form of gun licence revenue amounting to over a million pounds a year. Eighty per cent of sportsmen take out a licence principally to shoot rabbits, which are protected by law, and may only be taken from September 1st to the first Sunday in January.

Bills were introduced into the French Assembly to make the introduction and use of myxomatosis illegal. But the test case against Delille was to fail on a technicality – it could not be proved that the virus had been introduced into the affected rabbitry directly by the defendant. Later Delille was to receive a gold medal from the Académie d'Agriculture; but he has not ceased to be execrated by rabbit fanciers and hunters.

During our visit to France we were surprised to find that some of the biologists working on myxomatosis whom we interviewed had found out very little about the vectors of the disease in France, but had accepted stories that the virus was transmitted across country by various agencies of direct contact, particularly on the wheels of cars which had run over myxomatous rabbits. Dr P. Lépine of the Pasteur Institute cited to us the case of a sportsman, returning from shooting in the Sologne in central France where the disease was rife, who left his hunting equipment (boots and game bag) in the rabbitry at his home in Alsace more than one hundred miles distant from the nearest epidemic. Ten days later the rabbits in his hutches contracted myxomatosis; this was the first outbreak in eastern France, from which it spread subsequently into Germany.

By the autumn of 1953 myxomatosis crossed the Channel into Sussex and Kent. On behalf of the Nature Conservancy I investigated the outbreak. As a farmer I could listen sympathetically to local landowners whom I interviewed in the affected parishes. They advised me to help myself to sick rabbits – thinking that this is what, like other farmers who came to see them, I wanted. As none admitted introducing the disease it seemed possible to me that the infection reached England naturally by way of fleas attaching to a migrating bird which had fed upon the carcase of a myxomatous rabbit in Northern France.

My first examinations of myxomatous rabbits in that autumn and winter in Sussex and Kent proved that these were heavily parasitised by the rabbits' natural flea *Spilopsyllus cuniculi*. This flea easily transferred to human hands and clothing when the carcases were handled. Even when the rabbit had been dead for a week I found some fleas remained alive and congregated in the fur between the body and the ground; their powers of survival in this situation were considerable, even in frost and under snow. I noticed that the last rabbits to remain alive in a myxomatous warren were swarming with hundreds of fleas, and probably this burden had been acquired by the movement of hungry fleas from the dead to the living rabbit in a chain migration.

This set me wondering if the flea was the vector of the virus, Remembering Dr Lépine's story I made a simple test. I found that when I placed rabbits, alive or freshly dead, in a game bag, some of the fleas dropped off and remained at the bottom of the bag. Could Dr Lépine's sportsman have been instrumental in transferring the infection unknowingly from infected Sologne rabbits to the rabbits in hutches in Alsace? Had the infected fleas from the Sologne hopped or crawled from his game bag or boots on to the domestic rabbits against the hutches of which these articles had been hung by the sportsman?

It would be easy to try out a similar experiment. I collected fleas from dead or dying rabbits in Sussex. They survived well, in test tubes packed with rabbit fur and unmedicated cottonwool, when transported over 100 miles to a research laboratory. Here they were placed on healthy domestic rabbits in hutches or upon wild rabbits in small outdoor enclosures.

The results are summarised in the accompanying table (page 122). These experiments were published in the Veterinary Record (Lockley, 1954). I proved by these tests that the rabbit flea is able to survive at least six days in cold weather upon the carcase of a rabbit in the field after the death of its host, and is also capable of carrying the virus over this period, plus a further two days under artificial conditions. The numbers of fleas which were used to convey the virus successfully to seven individual rabbits were 25, 29, 25, 23, 12, 10, and 6. In three other tests with groups of 4, 3 and 1 fleas respectively the virus was apparently not conveyed; no disease developed.

In one experiment I found that many fleas migrated from the fur of a freshly killed wild rabbit to that of a domestic rabbit in whose hutch the carcase had been placed. This was indicative of what happened when a wild rabbit died in an inhabited burrow.

A tame buck with myxomatosis remained remarkably vigorous to within a few days of its death, and attempted to mate with a healthy doe in spite of his blindness and swollen genitals, and the passive (non-oestrous) behaviour of the doe. (This suggested that the buck was not in much pain from the repulsive-looking disease.) Although this buck rubbed his purulent head over the doe's fur and even scratched at her with his sharp claws and bit her in his attempt to stimulate her to a successful copulation, the doe did not contract myxomatosis from these rough contacts.

These and other experiments showed that the flea was a highly successful vector of myxomatosis in Britain, and contact between sick and healthy rabbits was only important for the transfer of infected fleas. (See table on following page.)

The Ministry of Agriculture had meanwhile conducted experiments to test the effectiveness of British mosquitoes as vectors. Hutches containing healthy domestic rabbits were hung on trees a few feet from the ground in wild rabbit warrens in which myxomatosis was rife, and *Aëdes* mosquitoes (which bite man) observed to frequent the burrows. The wild rabbits died out, but the domestic rabbits remained healthy; it was evident that British

Rabbit Flea as Vector of the Myxoma Virus. Summary of Experiments. 1954.

Experiment No.	Date Original Host died	Date and Number of Fleas collected		Date and Number of Fleas transmitted		New Host Domestic (D) Wild (W) Male (M) Female (F)	Interval before death from Myxomatosis
AD	9th Jan	15th Jan	35	17th Jan	29	ad.m(D)	12 days
BE	14th Jan	16th Jan	12	17th Jan	12	ad.f.(D)	13 days
CP	16th Jan	16th Jan	4	17th Jan	4	ad.f.(D)	survived
G	25th Mar	25th Mar	10	27th Mar	10	ad.f.(D)	12 days
H	25th Mar	25th Mar	35	27th Mar	25	imm.(D)	12 days
I	22nd Apr	23rd Apr	23	23rd Apr	23	4 imm. (W)	c. 12 days
J	25th Mar	25th Mar	25	28th Mar	25	imm.f.(W)	11 days
K	8th Apr	9th Apr	6	9th Apr	6	ad.m.(D)	13 days
L	8th Apr	5th Apr	3	5th Apr	3	ad.f.(D)	survived
M	8th Apr	5th Apr	1	5th Apr	1	ad.m.(D)	survived

mosquitoes were, in general, ineffective, that fleas do not normally climb trees (or that hungry fleas are insensitive to the presence of a suitable host hung up on trees.) Generally, fleas are considered to be photonegative – they seek darkness; however, rabbit fleas, clinging for preference for much of their adult lives to the ears of their host, are evidently resistant to light during the period the rabbit is living above ground.

The reason why the virus failed when introduced at Skokholm by Sir Charles Martin eighteen years earlier was now discovered. There are no rabbit fleas on Skokholm (Lockley 1955) but why there are none on that island, and plenty on the island of Skomer, two miles distant, is not known. Myxomatosis has since ravaged Skomer Island, but never Skokholm. Sir Charles Martin's choice of Skokholm for his experiments in 1936 was therefore a most unlucky chance.

After its first appearance in late 1953 in Kent and East Sussex, myxomatosis was reported to be making leaps over hundreds of miles into Wales, Scotland and even Ireland early in 1954 in the manner of outbreaks of foot-and-mouth disease. But by now I was convinced that these new isolated outbreaks were not due, as some reports suggested, to infection carried by migratory birds on their spring travels, or by flying insects. They must be due to artificial methods.

Early in May I spent some time investigating the very first and isolated outbreaks in the Cotswolds and Radnorshire. Again, using my name as a farmer, I quickly ascertained that the disease had been introduced by local landowners and by farmers who had made special journeys to obtain dying or dead rabbits from the infected warrens in Sussex or Kent. They hospitably took me to their own now infected warrens so that we could obtain infective material.

During a discussion on 'myxy', as the disease was popularly called, while lunching at the bar of a Radnorshire inn there was the usual good-humoured controversy between one or two farmers and farm workers. The latter bemoaned the loss of the rabbit as the labourers' perquisite, and accused the landowner of robbing the poor man of his standby for Sunday dinner. One workman gleefully related how his boss had travelled 200 miles there and back to collect myxomatous rabbits from Kent, but the disease had failed to appear.

'How did the rabbits survive the journey?' I asked.

'They was stone cold when we took 'em out of the car,' he replied.

'Did you notice any fleas alive on the rabbits?'

'Fleas? Didn't bother to look. Boss dumped the dead rabbits down holes in different burrows.'

At that moment a car arrived and the man's boss walked in. He stood the company drinks, and over them confirmed what his employee had said. He couldn't understand the failure, but was going to get some fresh 'myxy' rabbits from a nearby friend whose land was now covered with dying rabbits.

I found out why his attempt had failed. He had put the dying rabbits in the boot of his car. They had died within an hour. Business in London prevented him from getting back home immediately. The dead rabbits remained in the car for three days before he could insert them in burrows on his own land.

'During that time,' I told him 'all the fleas would have left or been shaken off the body, and they are probably at this moment in the bottom of the boot of your car. Shall we go and look?'

We found many dead and a few live fleas in the layer of dirt and debris usually found in the bottom of the boot of a farmer's car which is commonly used for conveying sacks and tools. I placed some thirty of the surviving fleas on rabbit fur in a test tube.

'We'll see,' I said, 'if these are still infective.'

On getting to my house that afternoon, by pure coincidence I was met by a deputation of monks from a religious house situated on a remote island. They knew me as a naturalist and had heard that I was engaged on research into the vectors of myxomatosis. Their mission was to get advice on how to introduce the disease on their rabbit-ridden island farm.

'We have turned down hundreds of cats,' said the steward monk who acted as spokesman, 'but they have failed – they just live on wild birds and kill our pheasants. We are no longer permitted by law to use steel gin-traps. And there are no weasels, stoats or foxes. We have shot and ferreted but with no success. Our last resort is myxomatosis. How do we get it started?'

'After you have killed a sick rabbit, just cut off the ears if these are full of fleas, as they usually are, and transfer them in a flea-tight container to an inhabited warren on your island. That is, if you really must make the experiment.'

I showed them the test-tube containing the fleas (originating in Sussex) which had become lively in the warmth of my pocket.

'Ah – can we try these? It would save a lot of trouble?' said the businesslike spokesman monk.

'But how long do they remain infective?' asked another.

'Those fleas have been in the bottom of a car for nearly a month,' I said, 'and they are dying off hourly for lack of food. I doubt if they are much use.' Then I added, half seriously, half teasingly, 'You know, of course, that myxomatosis is a horrible-looking disease? And frankly we are amazed at men of God proposing to introduce a disgusting disease into your beautiful island. But then you monks have unusual ideas. Your pig scheme . . .'

We had never approved of the way this community of monks had introduced pigs to plough up the cliffs and commons of their island, which had once been so wondrously coloured with wild flowers and alive with sea birds. The pigs had been one of the 'phases' in their farming enthusiasm which changed periodically with fluctuations in profitability of farm produce, and was now concentrated on producing roast chicken and boudoir scent from a curious combination of a broiler farm and a herb garden. Visitors to the island could buy roast fowl and a bottle of scent after paying their landing fee.

'Money!' sighed the steward. 'Alas, we need to make money for the rebuilding of our monastery church which burnt down and was uninsured. Besides we still have a debt to repay our mother house for the capital purchase of the island.'

'And rabbits, like pigs and chickens, have no souls!' announced one monk who had been silent all this time.

The argument went no further. The monks, and the fleas, went to the island. The fleas were ineffective, which suggested that a month was too long for the virus to remain viable on the mouth parts of this vector.

The steward later informed me that fresh fleas taken from the ears of myxomatous mainland rabbits and introduced the same day in burrows on the island successfully started an epidemic which swept the rabbits away, and they were now engaged in shooting the starving cats instead!

The role of the rabbit flea *Spillopsyllus cuniculi* as the most important vector of myxomatosis in Britain has encouraged attempts to introduce it into countries where it is absent, and where myxomatosis as a result is wholly or partially ineffective, such as the dry areas of Australia and the whole of New Zealand.

In these countries wild rabbits were first introduced from Europe in the days of sailing ships, just over one hundred years ago. During the long voyages which lasted several months the fleas are not likely to have survived the conditions of living in hutches. In Australia the native stickfast flea, *Echidrophaga myrmecobii*, can convey the virus between sick and healthy rabbits, but it is not effective for large-scale epidemics, probably because it does not infest rabbits heavily, but only casually as a wanderer from its natural marsupial host, the kangaroo.

Until recently nothing was known about the rabbit flea, except that it infested chiefly the ears of rabbits, where it clung with mouth parts embedded in the skin. Attempts to breed the flea under controlled conditions failed until A. R. Mead-Briggs (1960) discovered that the ovaries of the female flea do not mature and she will not lay fertile eggs until she has fed on blood from a pregnant doe. In the warmth of the nursery nest prepared by the doe prior to parturition the female flea, having gorged on the pregnant doe's blood, leaves her host in order to deposit fertile eggs in the nest. The larval flea when hatched feeds at first on the debris in the bottom of the burrow, including the droppings (containing residual rabbit's blood) from the mother flea or from those of other fleas which have been feeding on rabbit blood; when adult it climbs upon the body of the nearest rabbit, be it the doe, her kittens, or other rabbits which frequent the burrow in which it was hatched, and attaches itself, feeding and wandering about its host.

Rabbit fleas are most numerous on the ears of rabbits in the months of the main pregnancy period of the does, from January to June. The fertile eggs hatch rapidly in warm weather and the young fleas are spread throughout the colonies during the breeding season by the movement of both young and old rabbits. Older rabbits tend to accumulate larger numbers of fleas than young ones; and some weanling kittens have no fleas. The numbers of fleas decline by natural loss in late summer and autumn when the female fleas are infertile through lack of pregnant doe blood to feed on.

Myxomatosis, carried far and wide by land-users in the British Isles, from Land's End to John o' Groats and even the Shetland Isles, has reduced rabbit populations from their formidable pre-1954 numbers to what seems to be a low degree of infestation, an equilibrium resembling that of rabbit numbers early in the nineteenth century. This was the period, which had lasted since the introduction of rabbits in Norman times, of some 700 years during which the rabbit was never a serious menace to agriculture and forestry. It was kept in check by natural predators and by a countryside more heavily populated than it is today with farm labourers and country artisans who caught them legally or illegally, chiefly for food. For hundreds of years the wild rabbit was scarce enough to be protected by a close season, as it is in France today; and was bred for profit, in enclosed warrens on sandy soil, and was sold for food and fur.

The Ground Game Act of 1880 gave tenants the right to take rabbits on their farms. On small farms rabbits began to be regarded as rent payers, and even, in years of high prices, as profitable crops. Rabbit-farming on small farms, in West Wales and Cornwall in particular, became an industry with the commercial production of the steel trap, the four-inch wide saw-edged spring gin which, laid under earth or grass covering, in the rabbits' hole or runway, catches the rabbit by one or two legs – and usually breaks them. It is an excessively cruel device, and the rabbit screams in agony; it remained in the trap all night until the trapper made his morning round.

Such a trap, often set in the open, caught many other animals, especially the natural predators of the rabbit: fox, badger, polecat, stoat, weasel, as well as domestic cats, dogs, wild birds and game-birds. These comprised about ten to fifteen per cent of the daily catch. The trapper was in effect killing or maiming the natural controls; and this suited his business, which was to eliminate the rabbits' enemies and leave a strong nucleus of rabbits to breed and provide a bigger crop next season.

Rats also increased as foxes, stoats and weasels declined. It is safe to say that the introduction of the steel rabbit trap led to the huge increase of rabbits and rats in the British Isles in the first half of the present century, which caused intolerable damage to agricultural production of cereals, kale, roots and grass crops, damage estimated, in the twenty-five years up to 1953, to be at the rate of some forty to fifty million pounds annually. Against this the direct income from rabbits received by agriculture was only about two million pounds a year, excluding the trade in by-products such as fur and felt, carried on by manufacturers.

With the arrival of myxomatosis in 1953 the sudden loss of interest in rabbit-meat by the consuming public practically exterminated the market in rabbits for several years. At the same time rabbit numbers were to drop to possibly one-tenth of their former high level. Although hundreds of trappers were out of work (about half the population of Anglesey depended on rabbits for their living at the time) the benefit to agriculture was immediately apparent. And these trappers became reabsorbed into farming and other rural industries.

In 1954 the Pests Act was passed, making the use of the gin-trap illegal after July, 1958. This Act was the result of a long agitation by humanitarians and also by far-seeing farmers and other land-users who recognised that the gin had encouraged the spread of the rabbit. It was a fortunate moment – as rabbit traps and the rabbit-trapping trade died out, myxomatosis took over, far more effectively, the control of the rabbit.

Myxomatosis has kept rabbit numbers low ever since. As the disease died out for lack of material to feed upon, it was revived, generally artificially, in areas where rabbits had built up in numbers again. It still survives. It seems to have become enzootic, that is, an endemic disease in Britain, permanent and varying in virulence, as is influenza in man. It is still spread by man, but it is evidently not completely dependent on artificial distribution for its survival; even in areas of low density it reappears sporadically.

Its virulence is still high, often as high as the original 99% lethality; but in some local epidemics the death-rate is lower, nearer 50%. The rabbit is slowly acquiring immunity, or the virus is weakening in virulence, or both; as in Australia.

Meanwhile, in the absence of rabbit gins, which destroyed them, the numbers of predatory animals have slowly recovered their ancient strength. It was thought that these – foxes, stoats and weasels especially – would have remained scarce for lack of their normal rabbit diet. But it is now obvious that these predators can thrive among low populations of rabbits, as in centuries past, and in fact can help to keep rabbits numbers low – except where gamekeeping interests destroy these predators.

It has been remarked that rats also have become much scarcer since myxomatosis and the banning of the gin-trap, probably for the same reasons.

And what of the future?

Myxomatosis has had a most beneficial effect on the agricultural economy. It can never exterminate the rabbit completely. It has in fact restored the rabbit to its former smaller numbers, approaching a healthy equilibrium with its natural predators. We now believe that if myxomatosis dies out in Britain, or eventually becomes a non-lethal permanent disease (as in the Brazilian rabbit) and that if foxes, stoats and weasels are allowed to exist in their pre-gin-trap numbers, rabbits are never likely again to become a general widespread plague to land-users.

Farmers and foresters have seen the great benefits of the present rabbit scarcity. They have established Rabbit Clearance Societies covering most districts of the British Isles today. Members contribute money on an acreage basis, and the Ministry of Agriculture adds an equal contribution. Each Society employs a roving team of rabbit-catchers, using ferrets or gas or both (but not gin-traps) to deal with local infestations.

By the Rabbit Acts, 1955, New Zealand made rabbit control compulsory, and at the same time prohibited all trade in rabbit flesh and fur. This de-commercialisation and 'killer' policy has been completely successful. Trained professional men carry out the control by a system of visiting districts where rabbits are reported on the increase.

A somewhat similar system of control has been adopted in Australia, but some States are more lax than others, and the sale of rabbits is permitted; but wherever the rabbit is an article of commerce and profit it tends to become farmed rather than exterminated, with a return to conditions (obtaining before the advent of myxomatosis in the area) of deterioration of pasture and a fall in farm meat, milk and crop yields. Australians still have a serious rabbit problem.

It has been estimated, by acceptable methods of measurement, that the food requirements of a sheep weighing 120 lb are equal to those of ten rabbits (weight about 40 lb adult); in effect the sheep is three times as effective as the rabbit in converting pasture into meat, and in addition it is an improver of grassland by its even, non-selective grazing, where the rabbit despoils it by close-cropping of the best clovers and grasses, leaving behind woody unpalatable species. Before myxomatosis struck in west Wales, the production of rabbit meat (for example in 1945) was extremely high, and that of beef, veal, mutton and pig meat correspondingly low: it was estimated that in Pembrokeshire in that year rabbit meat production (trapped wild rabbits) was 1,460 tons, almost exactly half that of beef – 2,910 tons, and far exceeding that of veal – 352 tons, sheep – 557 tons, and pig – 190 tons. Exact figures for the post-myxomatosis period are not available, but in the years 1954 to 1963 practically no rabbit meat has left Pembrokeshire.

Many rabbit clearance societies forbid the sale of rabbits caught; and this should be made a law in all rabbit control areas, as in New Zealand, where farm production per acre is now the highest in the world. Domestic rabbits can still be bred, and (as in France for centuries past) can yield valuable white meat of high quality, as well as useful fur, to supply a keen demand for these products of hutched tame rabbits.

We are never likely to exterminate the rabbit in any country of the size of the British Isles, Australia, or New Zealand. The rabbit's capacity for breeding rapidly when its numbers are low, its resilient adaptability to climate and environment, have been described in this book. Nor would the majority of us wish to see the rabbit exterminated, any more than we would wish the fox and badger, the hedgehog and the hare to disappear.

The new system and humane methods of control by rabbit clearance societies fortunately seem to ensure that the rabbit will survive, along with its predators, as an attractive member of our countryside fauna, comparatively scarce and no longer a serious pest.

13 The Rabbit Wild and Free

'Twas dew-tide coming,
The turf was sweet
To nostril, curved tooth,
And wool-soft feet – WALTER DE LA MARE

From our own studies and from those of enclosure experiments (still continuing) in Australia it is possible to summarise our extensive new knowledge of the life history of the rabbit – knowledge of the social structure of rabbit society which might have been difficult to obtain without this form of experimental control. This chapter will attempt to review this information and apply it in generalised terms to the rabbit wild and free. Our summary is likely to be imperfect and incomplete; but then the last word in any research can never be said – there is always more to learn, and this is part of the joy of animal study.

By nature the wild rabbit is partial to open country with a well-drained, sandy soil in temperate zones. It avoids low-lying ground with dense vegetation and long grass. In Europe it is most numerous in regions of high sunshine, and mild winters. In such conditions it survives drought more easily than heavy rainfall; it is more easily drowned out than starved out. It avoids high mountain country if this is cold, with snow in winter. A mild coastal region with blown sand is a favourite habitat. It does not thrive in dense coniferous forest, but is found in deciduous woodland with light ground vegetation. A usual habitat is the edge of woodland bordering grass or arable land, where it has good dry cover to which it can retire from open grazing. It was formerly very numerous on open downland closely grazed by sheep in southern England, on dry chalk slopes with or without scrub cover. It found the stone-walled earth hedges of the mild hilly south-west farmland of England and Wales ideal for burrowing purposes, and was a serious pest to agriculture there until swept away by myxomatosis. But it does not succeed in flat intensively farmed, rotationally cropped land.

The wild rabbit is born blind and deaf and hairless in a nest made of soft dried vegetation lined with fur pulled by the doe from her belly. This helps to uncover her teats, which are usually eight in number, widely spaced along the belly. The new-born 'kitten' can crawl about at birth. It weighs under two ounces. In seven days it has more or less doubled its weight: the auditory system is completely developed about the eighth day, when its fur has grown to cover its nakedness, and the teeth and claws are visible, the former about one, and latter about two, millimetres long. The eyes are open before the tenth day.

In the warm, underground, almost airless nest the kitten's rate of respiration is approximately 100 per minute. The faeces are small, round, pale, yellowish, or greenish, and apparently are licked away by the doe during the period that the young are helpless. The nest is kept dry and clean. The week-old kitten's stomach contains clotted milk; and the large intestine already has the first seed-like soft pellets which later will be reingested when the kitten begins to run out and graze.

It is believed that the wild doe suckles her litter only at night, opening the earth covering the nest for a short period once (or rarely twice) during twenty-four hours. As the litter grows in bulk the kittens begin pushing their way to the surface, and the doe ceases to cover the nursery over with earth once they emerge, at sixteen to twenty-one days of age. Some 'stops', especially those of a queen doe, buried deep in a large warren, have little earth over them.

The kittens begin to graze after a day or two of cautious peeping at the burrow entrance. Before they are a month old they are able to run about and play together within a few yards radius of the burrow entrance. To this they retreat on the appearance of danger, which behaviour is apparently learned rather than instinctive though probably a mixture of both. The doe, usually close at hand or on watch at this three to four week period, warns her kittens of danger by stamping her hind feet on the ground and elevating her white scut. They precede or follow her below ground, amusingly copying her signals with stamping feet and raised tails!

This early lesson in danger is most important, as unless the litter is the last of the season, the doe abandons them during the fourth week. She has mated two days after the birth of the litter and is now about to give birth to the next litter, and must prepare another nest, usually in a separate burrow dug within her warren or, if she is a secondary doe, in an altogether different site.

The abandoned kittens are not dependent for food on the doe. They are already grazing at three weeks of age; and reingesting the soft pellets. They are already trained to run to cover at sight or sound of predatory animals, including bird, cat and man. They remain a little longer in the nesting burrow; and during innocent play they establish, like children, their own leader, and social order or hierarchy. The strong individual pushes the weaker out of its way; gradually playfulness develops into aggressiveness, although this is in a mild form as yet, and is due as much to the congested state of the nursery burrow, as to their various degrees of natural ebullience, according to age and health.

The young kittens during their second month of life gradually disperse, the subordinates occupying outlying holes in the home warren, or in summer lying out in long grass or other shelter in the open. Much depends on the state of the warren – if this is congested the young rabbits are pushed outwards; if almost empty, as after an epidemic disease or from other causes, the young ones will remain close to home, taking over disused burrows and bolt holes.

In this season of late summer and early autumn the life of the wild rabbit is almost carefree, with plenty of food and cover. The warren is a hive of expanded population scattered around the queen or matriarch at the heart of the community.

The children of the dominant or queen doe at the centre have the advantage of being brought up in the best quarters and under the protection of the most powerful buck and doe. They are tolerated by their parents in the neutral season of non-breeding in the late summer, and as long as they remain submissive and there is room for them they can stay in the commodious central palace.

But there is often no room in the palace burrows for the youngsters born to subordinate does in nursery stops outside the centre warren. Whilst their natural gregariousness tends to draw them towards the bustling centre warren, it will depend on the degree of density there whether or not they are able to find an empty niche, a burrow or bolt hole unoccupied by the royal family and the royal entourage of 'familiars' – relatives, children and perhaps grandchildren of the king buck and his queen.

Nevertheless, even in a crowded centre warren, visitors in the form of young rabbits seeking desirable dry quarters may be tolerated in the neutral season, July to late September, and if powerful enough they may obtain and hold a place later in the autumn when territoriality is renewed with the development of sexual activity and libido.

Even the older bucks, which had fought during the breeding season, may rest together side by side in the same burrow during the off-season; but usually each remains in his own burrow. In fact this period of moult, over the three late summer months July to September inclusive, is a season of complete armistice, when sociability replaces territoriality and hostility. Like the moulting stags of the deer herds, which have cast their antlers, the buck rabbits, their fur in moult and their testes withdrawn, are indifferent to sex; but we do not find the sexes are segregated as in deer in moult.

This season of armistice is biologically significant. The royal family at the centre, lately dominated by the most powerful, generally the oldest, buck and doe, with children and grandchildren (some may be step-children of a new king or queen) are relaxed and mixed together, with possibly a leavening of visiting strangers from less desirable physically inferior warrens and nursery burrows nearby. This ensures that such new blood as is available in the district is brought into contact with the (possibly inbred) royal line, that the most powerful of the young visiting bucks (and some may be older experienced breeding males) will have the opportunity to contest the leadership of the warren with the late king and other aspirants to the kingship and inject their virile blood into the community.

Generally the young buck of the year has little chance of achieving a dominant position before he has experienced a winter (breeding season) as a subordinate. But if he is strong and virile, which he is likely to be if he is a son and intimate of the king or queen or both, and born early in the year in a large royal warren he has obviously a better chance of securing a mate, possibly a sister, in the precincts and settling down to breed in some secondary burrow of the main labyrinth, before he is a year old. If the first born he is also more powerful, and larger than the kittens of later royal litters.

The young buck displays his virility by various displacement activities as described in Chapter 3, such as mock-fighting, aggressive attitudes, digging little scrapes, and 'chinning' his territory with scent. This activity is probably part instinctive, part learned from the adult. The young female behaves passively by comparison, although she too will dig scrapes, and frisk playfully in apparent high spirits.

The maturing kitten under pressure from increasing numbers and the competition of its elders and contemporaries is compelled to live on the perimeter of the colony. In late summer and early autumn it lies out in the open, squatting like a hare in a form, pressed and nibbled to shape in long grass or low cover. It is exiled, and footloose.

Like young animals of many species, the young rabbit wanders farthest during its first year of independence, partly due to the hostility of the other rabbits and partly because it has no sexual ties at this stage of its life. Thus the young Atlantic seal becomes solitary and wanders farthest in its first winter, swimming hundreds of miles and not returning home until adolescence and the first physical intimations of maturity awaken its interest in its fellow seals. Seal and rabbit make a suitable comparison, as both are gregarious, less so than deer and sheep, more so than bear or fox, for example. Many birds behave similarly, by wandering solitary for a year or more, making their longest migrations over the year (or two) before they attain sexual maturity. It is these youngsters which found new colonies.

The wild doe rabbit in Europe does not usually reach sexual maturity until it is between nine and twelve months old. But if born early in winter, and given ideal feeding and territorial conditions the young doe is known to breed earlier, producing one, rarely two, litters during its first summer; this is recorded frequently in New Zealand and Australia in certain years under favourable weather conditions. The young doe may then breed at five or six months of age, but the young buck is not fertile until nine or ten months old.

The wild rabbit in the British Isles attains its heaviest weight and presumably its best condition when it is about twenty months old, after its first breeding season is over, and its second winter is approaching. A decline in weight sets in after the twentieth month (Fig 14).

During the first winter of its life, especially if it is born late in the spring, the young rabbit (six to twelve months) weighs about one-third less than the mature eighteen months old rabbit. It is often thin or without fat in the body cavity, and it is more susceptible to disease than the mature adult.

Under pressure of population at the centre these thin young rabbits, the lowest in the hierarchy of the colony, must move out if they are to survive.

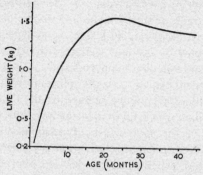

FIGURE 14. Average live weights of 100 wild rabbits at Orielton

In a wild and free state they are the individuals which stray sometimes for miles but usually for shorter distances, during late autumn and early winter, wandering until they find a suitable undisturbed environment with food and cover. Depending on the quality of these essentials of quiet, food and shelter, as well as on the presence of other rabbits which will satisfy their natural gregariousness and rising sexual need or libido, the young rabbits eventually settle in a suitable spot and dig new burrows, or occupy old deserted warrens. If they wander into an unsuitable environment they may die from various causes, especially predators.

One can observe in nature how a pair of rabbits will appear in a new situation – a hedgebank, the edge of a wood, a disused burrow on downland – and feed together evening after evening. Within a few weeks of the spring flush of grass the first kittens appear at the burrow entrance. If this nucleus remains undisturbed, more burrows and bolt holes are dug or reopened, and the new colony – a matriarchy – is firmly established by the late summer. The original (queen) doe will nurse from two to five or six litters in the warren, digging a new nest site for each within the enlarging burrow.

It is always the doe who initiates the new colony. She it is who, under compulsion of her rapidly developing pregnancy, digs the initial burrow, sometimes a few feet, sometimes several yards long, and sets up the home and underground shelter which she and her children need, but which her mate also adopts. The mated buck is an idle character when it comes to burrowing; at most he scratches perfunctorily for a short time as if to enlarge the new warren for his own convenience, or perhaps merely for exercise. But he rarely spends more than a few minutes at this task. His main pre-occupation, aside from feeding and lazing, is to defend the home and grazing territory adopted by his doe, to mate with her, and to protect her from other rabbits, especially libidinous males.

We have described (Chapter 11) the phenomenon of resorption of embryos, the prenatal mortality of one or more or all of the developing litter in the womb of the doe, which takes place at any time from half-term to three-quarters term of the four weeks of pregnancy. Students of this phenomenon find that resorption may be highest in young does, that many of the first litters of these inexperienced breeders are resorbed entirely during the second or third week; and it is also believed that resorption is as much a psychological as a physiological reaction to adverse factors in the environment.

One might argue that resorption of the first litter of a young doe can be a convenient device. In starting a home of her own the pregnant young doe could be seriously handicapped if her choice of the environment proved later to be unsuitable by some new disturbance as, for instance, by the arrival of predators, by the attention of man (ferreting and destruction of burrows) determined to destroy the colonists, even by adverse weather such as snow or drought. Such disturbance might alarm the pregnant doe, and thus trigger off the resorption process.

Under adverse conditions such as these (and in crowded colonies similar psychosis or psycho-physiological stress can induce resorption) the young doe may completely reabsorb the embryos and placental tissues internally without abortion within two or three days. The onset of oestrous behaviour after a complete resorption was found by Myers and Poole (1962) to be (with some variation) approximately one month from the period of first conception; that is to say, the doe mates at any time from a few days after the resorption. Thus a doe could conceive twice in one month, yet produce no young until the environmental conditions were favourable. False pregnancy (pseudo-pregnancy) is also recorded frequently; after sexual stimulation without fertilisation, ovulation may occur; the breasts swell and produce milk, but the womb remains empty.

The doe's fecundity, in terms of live young produced, is apparently governed almost automatically by conditions of environment. As shown in our experiments, the idyllic conditions of abundant range and food in the extensive enclosure Savanna resulted in uninhibited breeding. This explains the rapidity with which rabbits often increase in a favourable environment newly colonised by them. Resorption is then low or nil.

As already mentioned, Myers and Poole also found that older females, which had resorbed one or more first litters, were less liable to resorb later litters, which were also larger than those produced by young does at corresponding stages of the season. In other words, as does became mature, dominant and settled in the best breeding sites, they became less nervous, more fertile, and more adapted to the environmental conditions.

Normally, in good weather and food conditions, the wild buck is ready to mate in October; and the doe is able to produce a litter approximately every thirty days between November and June under the same ideal conditions of food and climate. Pregnancies are most frequent from February to May in the British Isles, suggesting that does are later than bucks in becoming fertile. The normal litter is four to six; thus a fertile doe could produce thirty or more young in a season. The daughters of her first litter, born November to January, could have one or two litters late in the summer. A single fertile adult doe could be, under perfect conditions, the mother or grandmother of up to forty kittens in one breeding season.

In New Zealand, Watson (1954) found some does were pregnant at any time of the year, but there was a well-defined main breeding season of five months, and breeding earlier or later than this was often unsuccessful due to resorption and climatic factors. He found that a fertile adult doe, under favourable conditions, could be mother or grandmother of up to sixty kittens in a year.

Sometimes a doe's milk will fail, as in sudden drought conditions, and the last born litter then starves to death. Green food is essential both to milk-production, and to fertility.

The tame buck and doe in the hutch, fed on greenstuff and stimulating artificial food, are known to be ready to mate at almost any time of the year, although there is a less fertile and less libidinous period in early autumn. But the fertility of the wild buck has a seasonal cycle; it declines rapidly in late summer; the buck becomes sterile (perhaps impotent) during the moult at that time, when his testes become flaccid and withdrawn. Severe weather conditions, particularly drought, also cause testicular regression and the disappearance of libido. But the doe is not necessarily infertile (anoestrous) at this time.

Male rather than female infertility therefore may determine the end of the breeding season and be the cause of failure of mature does to conceive at the off-season of the year and in droughts. Myers and Poole, as already cited, report a cycle of sexual behaviour in wild does occurring at seven-day intervals both before and during pregnancy. Towards the end of each seven-day period, the doe may actively solicit the buck, if the buck is indifferent. The occurrence of regular oestrous behaviour cycle of seven days in female rabbits appears, however, to be dependent on extraneous stimulations of a psychological nature initiated by the presence of males (and possibly homosexually by other females). This is in line with the natural behaviour reported of woman in primitive tribes in the presence of man (with, possibly, homosexuality stimulated when no men are present among several women). It is also reported in the sheep and the house mouse.

The readiness of the female to mate at all times when stimulated by the male has considerable survival value. Male infertility occurs in late summer and winter when grassland is dried up by summer drought, and litters of kittens, if born then, would die for lack of milk. The periodic long droughts experienced in Australia, which may last for more than a year, are, it is thought, responsible for the movements of hungry and thirsty rabbits across hundreds of miles of that continent. When the flush of new green grass occurs there is rapid development of fertility in the bucks, followed shortly after by almost simultaneous oestrus in the does, leading to a fall of litters on or about the same day. There is a nutritional factor here, as if the juices of green growing plants were essential to the diet before fertile matings take place.

The tendency for all the does to mate on or about the same day in these conditions may incidentally give the subordinate bucks the opportunity to share in paternity, since it is presumed that the dominant bucks are fully engaged in fertilising their 'queens', and will leave subordinate does alone.

In the event of sudden extremely unfavourable weather reversing the spring-like conditions, and reverting to arid drought, as sometimes though rarely happens, the stress resulting to the pregnant doe could trigger off prenatal mortality; this would then be followed by mating at the next oestrus a few days after resorption was complete. Breeding would be resumed but until the grass was green again few or no litters might be carried to full term.

This appears to be the pattern, explaining the remarkable resilience of the rabbit under varying external conditions. The elastic mechanism of its reproduction, and its social organisation, are such as to produce an immediate adaptation to conditions favourable for expansion, as well as to the pressures leading to reduction or stability of population. This is not a new discovery or observation; it is as old as the hills, and it must apply in greater or less degree to all surviving species. One is only looking anew at the behaviour which has made the rabbit an admirable success in nature; other mammals persecuted by man have succumbed, but the rabbit seems to have all the answers to its population problems, natural and man-made.

What part does natural predation play in the control of rabbit numbers? Many species of animals are recorded as preying on the rabbit. Foxes, dingos, wolves, coyotes, lynx, wolverine, and dogs will kill adult and young rabbits, chiefly by stalking and surprising them in the open, but in fact these predators are relatively unsuccessful – the rabbit usually gets to cover with a spurt of speed (with perhaps some twists and turns which are too quick for the pursuer to follow). Fox and badger dig out kittens from shallow nesting stops when they can find them; the badger is much too slow to catch a rabbit in any other way. Wild cats, which are rare today, and domestic cats, stalk and leap upon rabbits, taking them by surprise, especially young kittens when these leave the nest-stops at a tender age. The majority of domestic cats are not powerful enough to catch, hold and kill a healthy full-grown rabbit, although they will drag home a weak, diseased one.

Healthy adult rabbits can defend themselves with slashing teeth, but more usually with powerful kicking feet armed with needle-sharp claws. We have seen nursing does drive large cats away from nesting stops where young kittens were living. The doe will, it is said, successfully defend her weanlings even against ferret, stoat or weasel; she seems endowed with a fierce maternal strength. But usually she will run from these mustelids, which kill full-grown rabbits, although weasels are in fact seldom seen to kill strong, mature individuals.

Parties of stoats are said to hunt together, working rabbit burrows and intercepting the fleeing rabbits at several exits to the warren at the same time.

The same habit of hunting in a pack is recorded of weasels. I have never seen these foraging parties actually at work, but I have encountered small family parties of stoats (or of weasels), parent and young, on the move. Nor have I seen stoat or weasel performing what has been described as the 'dance of death', several times recorded in country periodicals: the mustelid gambols and rolls on the ground, attracting spectator birds and even rabbits to draw near out of curiosity – then suddenly it leaps at, catches and kills the nearest sightseer. It is certainly true that the presence of predatory hawk, owl, fox, cat, stoat, weasel, dog or other mammal often attracts the attention of local birds, which follow it, uttering alarm cries, but invariably keeping a safe distance.

Few birds can carry off an adult rabbit, even if they can kill it. Larger eagles, such as the golden eagle and sea eagle, can fly with a full-grown rabbit to their nests, but though small eagles, buzzards, and harriers will kill grown rabbits they cannot lift them without great difficulty; while hawks and owls can generally only manage to carry off quite small kittens, on which they prey freely. Ravens, crows, magpies and jays eat rabbits only as carrion on the ground, the result of death by another predator, by disease, or accident; in fact, one can see all kinds of animals, from rooks, rats, and hedgehogs, to dogs, foxes and beetles, feeding on rabbits killed on the roads by motor traffic.

Nevertheless there is no evidence that predators control the numbers of their prey; they are rather themselves controlled by the numbers of their prey. Like the rabbits which increase in an environment of plentiful food, predators tend to be numerous in proportion to the abundance of their food-prey. To maintain the food-chain of grass-eaten-by-rabbit-eaten-by-predator, all the components must survive in ratio that does not threaten any part with extinction. Thus buzzards were numerous in the rabbit-infested country of western England and Wales until myxomatosis reduced the rabbits to a fraction per cent of their previous numbers (during the rabbit-trapping era). In the first nesting seasons after myxomatosis few buzzards bred successfully; there was a decline in their numbers to match the new food situation of having to live on a non-rabbit diet. Rabbits are still comparatively rare in these western districts, but the buzzard survives in fair numbers without them.

Similarly it was thought that there would be a great decline in the population of the fox after myxomatosis. In fact it has greatly increased, and is obviously thriving on a non-rabbit diet. Personally, I put its increase down to the cessation of rabbit-trapping, which destroyed thousands of foxes annually.

Predators do have some effect on their prey, of course. It is a healthy one. They kill off the weaklings and the diseased first, because these are obviously the first to be caught. Elsewhere I have referred to the curious kind of paralysis which sometimes seizes a rabbit when a stoat or weasel pursues it. I have seen and heard a half-grown rabbit dragging its hind-legs feebly and screaming while a stoat was still a dozen feet away and approaching its victim at a gentle amble. This rabbit might already have been diseased, although it seemed to be quite healthy; I rescued it before the stoat reached it, but its eyes were already half-glazed, its heart violently palpitating, and its limbs trembling and unco-ordinated. It died within half an hour, apparently of heart attack on sighting or scenting the stoat. It is probable that rabbits have an innate fear of mustelids; but it must also be true that those weak enough to become paralysed at the moment of knowledge of pursuit by a mustelid will automatically be killed or die of fright. The elimination of these weaklings and the survival of the rabbits which are strong or astute enough to escape when so pursued is of benefit to the species; the

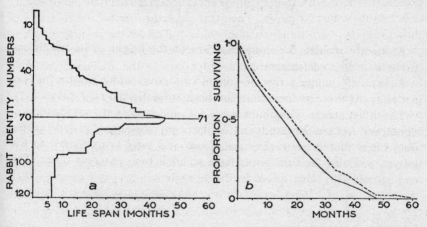

FIGURE 15. *a*, life-span data; complete records for nos. 1–70, incomplete for nos. 71–124. *b*, survivorship curves calculated: full line – without nucleus; pecked line – including nucleus.

ability to attempt to escape will be handed down, by instinct or learning or both, to the progeny of the survivors.

How long do rabbits live? If a population is stable, and the doe breeds when one year old (or a little earlier), she has only to produce two live young to adult stage to replace herself and the buck. The average life of the rabbit must thus be very short, not more than eighteen months, otherwise it would over-populate the land. But in fact the doe produces between, say, two and twenty live weanlings annually, with the severest mortality among the youngest age groups.

As a guide we may say that in our enclosure studies one or two rabbits were still alive at five years of age but the average expectation of life from the date of weaning was approximately one and a half years. Fig 15 shows the survivorship curve of 124 rabbits during the Orielton experiments. The survival rates of five age groups at the beginning of each breeding season (December) were:

At 8 months	42 per cent
At 20 months	73 per cent
At 32 months	55 per cent
At 44 months	35 per cent
At 56 months	nearly nil

At twenty months the individual was at the height of its health and strength in these enclosures.

In captivity, under protected conditions, a wild rabbit can live at least ten years. At that age domesticated rabbits are senile and rarely live longer.

The differences in life span between does and bucks were not found to be significant. At Orielton does up to the age of ten months tended to die earlier than bucks, but between the ages of two and three years tended to live longer, probably because bucks fight and kill each other at times. This corresponds with observations by other workers.

Sex Ratio

At weaning age there was a slight preponderance of females (100 males to 107 females) at Orielton. This is in line with figures before birth: Brambell

(1942) recorded 100:106 in 1,040 embryos between twenty-one days of gestation and full term; and Stephens (1952) gives prenatal sex ratios of 100:106. Figures for sexes of rabbits caught at random in the wild are unreliable because methods of catching may influence the result, unless all of the population is examined (as at Orielton). Present evidence is that the sex ratio in rabbits remains at about 100 males to 107 females throughout life.

In monogamous (sometimes polygamous, rarely polyandrous) man the sex-ratio at birth is close to parity, although census figures have shown that after great wars have killed off large numbers of males there is a tendency for more males than females to be born; the mechanism of this interesting adjustment phenomenon is not understood, but the curious result may be a generation of surplus males which do not match in age the previous generation of females made artificially surplus and deprived of marriage by war casualties. In primitive communities of men, as in rabbits, when males are killed off by fighting, the resulting surplus females are mated polygamously; but in Christian societies man-made laws usually forbid polygamous marriages, although these laws do not prevent promiscuous mating.

Rabbits have no marriage laws as such; but in their sexual relations buck and doe are tied to each other by a code of behaviour closely resembling that of man. Young rabbits play together innocently, like children, at first; then comes an adolescent period, with indiscriminate sexual pursuits without fertile mating – resembling those of young men and women. The young couple eventually settle in a burrow, often a poor one, but they will improve it, or move to a better one as their social standing in the community rises. The young woman is 'married' now, the young doe is a 'queen'. Under fair conditions, without severe pressures due to predators, over-population, or food shortage, the couple – human or rabbit – may remain united for the rest of their lives by their territorial allegiance to a home. If there is a surplus female or two around, the queen doe will not actively prevent the king having sexual relations with her or them, provided these secondary females do not enter her home, and she will only attack them if they obstruct her path when grazing near by; married man has a similar relationship, albeit more furtive and clandestine, if he takes a 'mistress'. But neither man nor buck will usually allow another male to approach his female sexually, if he can prevent it. He will fight for the sanctity of home, where the female provides the main bonds tying the male to a husbandly existence – warm, dry quarters and sexual satisfaction. In man, family 'togetherness' is also important, and it is tolerated by the father rabbit in much the same degree. Provided the young ones are docile they are welcome to stay at home and be treated affectionately as subordinate beings.

Rabbits are so human. Or is it the other way round – humans are so rabbit?

Appendix

1. *Distribution*

Rabbits and hares are classified in the order *Lagomorpha*, family *Leporidae*. Hares are usually larger than rabbits; they do not burrow and their young are born in the open, well covered with fur, eyes and ears open, and able to run from birth. The gestation period, however, is the same as that of the rabbit, twenty-eight to thirty days. There are over thirty species of hare; its distribution, like that of the rabbit, aided by introduction, is world wide.

There are twenty-five species of rabbits, as follows:

Oryctolagus : Europe, North Africa, with introductions in Australia, New Zealand, and elsewhere.

Pronolagus : Four species in South Africa, with longer tails than *Oryctolagus.*

Caprolagus : A dark-coated species found in Nepal, Assam and Northern India.

Nesolagus : A small mottle-coated species, Sumatra.

Pentalagus : A dark-coloured species. Liukiu Islands, Japan.

Silvilagus : Fifteen species, resembling European *Oryctolagus* but varying much in size. Tail short or very short. North, Central and South Americas and West Indies.

Brachylagus : A single species, Western North America.

Romerolagus : A small almost black species found on volcanic slopes of Mts Popocatapetl and Iztaccihuatl, Mexico. Rat-like, with small round ears and no visible tail.

The European *Oryctolagus cuniculus*, named by Linnaeus in 1758 as *Lepus cuniculus*, has been divided into races, doubtfully subspecific, as follows:

Oryctolagus cuniculus cuniculus, Linnaeus 1758: most of Europe except eastern, northern and alpine regions where snow lies for long periods in winter. Introduced Australia, New Zealand, Chile, Africa, and certain islands in Atlantic and Pacific.

Oryctolagus cuniculus huxleyi, Haekel 1874. Derived from *Oryctolagus cuniculus cuniculus*. Introduced on warm Atlantic islands, notably Madeira, Desertas, Salvage Islands, the Azores. Size varies from large hare-like individuals on Desertas to dwarf-sized specimens on Salvages.

Oryctolagus cuniculus brachyotus, Trouessart, 1917. Salt marshes of the Carmargue, Southern France.

In addition three races have been described from north-west Africa: *Oryctolagus cuniculus algirus*, Locke 1858, Algeria and Morocco; *Oryctolagus cuniculus oreas*, Cabrera 1922; and *Oryctolagus cuniculus Labetensis*, Cabrera 1923, both Spanish Morocco.

Mutations with peculiar colour and other abnormalities are recorded, especially in closed communities, as on small islands, where inbreeding occurs. Albinos are rather rare, but melanistic (black) are common and may form up to one hundred per cent of some communities (Islet of Samson, Isles of Scilly) but usually much less. A long-haired Angora-type is found on the islands of Skomer and Skokholm and rarely elsewhere. A typical 'Dutch-marked' variety is not uncommon; this has a white saddle and nose.

2. *Notes on Anatomy*

Rabbits and hares have chisel-like front teeth, with two pairs of upper incisors, distinguishing them from true rodents, such as rats and mice, which have only one pair. These upper incisors are powerful and consist of a large curved pair in front and a small pair reinforcing these behind. There are also three upper premolars, two lower premolars and three upper and three lower strongly ridged molars on each side of the jaw. The dental formula is

thus $\dfrac{2.\ 0.\ 3.\ 3.}{1.\ 0.\ 2.\ 3.} \times 2 = 28$ teeth. If broken or damaged in some way so that the upper and lower incisors do not meet and by continuous chisel action wear their sharp cutting edges down, these incisors will grow outward like tusks until the rabbit is unable to eat properly and dies of starvation.

The skeleton of the rabbit (Fig 16) shows the specialised cranium of a

SKELETON of RABBIT

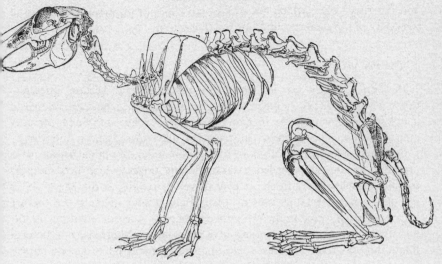

FIGURE 16. Skeleton of rabbit
Drawing by Peter Hurworth, from a specimen in the British Museum (Natural History) by courtesy of the Keeper of Zoology

herbivore, with dentition adapted to cutting down and grinding vegetation into fine particles. The eye socket is large to accommodate the large crepuscular eye. The powerful feet with sharp claws are not highly specialised, but are adapted to bounding escape flight, and to digging and shovelling earth during excavation. (However, the hare, which does not dig burrows, is similarly equipped with claws, and in both animals the claws come into play in fighting behaviour.)

The structure of the nostrils and scent glands indicate a high dependence on the sense of smell for identifying the individual rabbit and its sex, as well as enemies (page 39). Rabbits will be seen to wink open their nostrils when testing the air: the open nostrils exhibit a sensory pad which is the receptor for these scents. Chin glands produce the scent droplets which are rubbed on the ground, especially by the buck.

The stomach and intestinal system (Fig 13) are adapted for the ingestion of large quantities of vegetation quickly, resulting in the production and excretion of capsules (soft pellets) rich in bacteria, and of high nutritive and digestive value, which are swallowed whole ('reingested') at leisure in the safety of the underground burrow (page 103).

3. *Diseases and Parasites*

Domestic rabbits are known to be susceptible to certain diseases – tuberculosis, venereal, stomach and throat infections – which are related to if not identical with those in man. *Myxomatosis* (page 115) and prenatal mortality (resorption of embryos) (page 111) have already been discussed.

Coccidiosis is known to kill more wild rabbits than any other disease. It is produced by the single-celled parasite *Eimeria steidae*, which in some wild colonies attacks nearly forty per cent of young rabbits at the age of six to ten and a half weeks (Stephens 1952.) In populous colonies the pasture becomes heavily contaminated with the eggs or oocysts, resulting in the ingestion of a large amount of infective material in a short space of time. A single infected rabbit can evacuate upon the ground up to 55,000 oocysts in one day, as well as reingest a similar number in its soft pellets in the same space of time. The soft pellets are therefore a reservoir for the disease, which in its later stages produces a white veining or lesions in the liver. Older rabbits acquire a resistance while acting as carriers, and the disease is rarely fatal in thinly inhabited warrens.

Liver-fluke, *Fasciola hepatica* affects a varying percentage of rabbits in suitable damp areas inhabited by the intermediate host, the mud-loving snail *Limnaea truncaluta*; the rabbit may assist in the propagation of this parasite by acting as its final host in the absence of sheep (or cattle) producing the eggs which are passed in the faeces and so reach the snail once more. The flukes when numerous cause a degeneration or cirrhosis of the liver and the rabbit becomes thin and weak and may not survive.

Worms. Like most wild mammals rabbits are usually, often heavily, parasitised by stomach worms which produce gastritis and anaemia. The roundworm *Trichostrongylus retortaeformis* is recovered from young rabbits in greater lengths and containing more eggs than in adult rabbits. The reverse is true of the roundworms *Graphidium strigosum* and *Passalurus ambiguus*.

There are several tapeworms infesting the rabbit, particularly *Cittotaenia ctenoides* and *Cittotaenia denticulata*. Also *Cittotaenia pectinata*, and the larval forms of *Taenia serialis* and *Taenia fusiformis*. Tapeworms' eggs may be ingested by the rabbit through mites which act as intermediate hosts of the *Cittotaenia* worms. Stomach, liver, genitals, skin, and body cavity can be affected, resulting in large cysts or liver lesions well known to the dealer in rabbits. But resistance is built up as the rabbit becomes mature, and these lesions may become calcified and harmless.

Rabbit Control

In Britain rabbits have no close season. An occupier has the right to kill rabbits on his land (Ground Game Act, 1880). He may give authority to kill rabbits only to members of his household, persons in his ordinary service, and one other person who is *bona fide* employed by him for reward in taking rabbits. He need not hold a game licence but no one may use a shot-gun to kill rabbits without a gun licence, except in the curtilage or garden area around his house. Rifles and bullet guns require a Firearms Certificate.

By the Pests Act, 1954, the Minister of Agriculture may give notice to an occupier to destroy rabbits breeding or harbouring on his land. Failure to obey such a notice can incur a fine of up to £25 plus £5 a day for every day after conviction on which the failure continues. The simplest answer is to join the local Rabbit Clearance Society by paying the fees (five pence or less per acre of land occupied) and getting their team of experts to control your rabbits. This they may only legally do by approved methods: by ferreting, use of dogs, gassing, snaring with wire snares, netting and shooting. Any other methods are doubtfully successful. Traps should be avoided; gin traps are illegal. Rabbits can be brought under control by these methods which do not destroy many of the natural enemies of the rabbit.

Foxes, badgers, stoats, weasels, hawks and owls should be allowed to aid and abet rabbit control. No form of poison bait laid in the open has yet been proved very effective; and although poisoning is practised abroad it can be extremely dangerous, with serious consequences for other animals, including domestic animals—as already the extensive use on the land of insecticide and herbicide poisons and seed dressings has proved.

A Short Bibliography

BARNETT, S. A. (1958)—*J. Psychosom. Res.* 3 : 1

BRAMBELL, F. W. R. (1942)—*Pro. Roy. Soc. Lond.* 130 : 462

BRAMBELL, F. W. R. (1944)—*Pro. Roy. Soc. Lond.* 114:1

GRIFFITHS, M., & D. DAVIES (1963)—*J. Nutrition.* 80 : 171

HAYWARD, J. S. (1961)—*C.S.I.R.O. Wildl. Res.* 6 : 160

LLOYD, H. G. (1963)—*J. Anim. Ecol.* 32 : 549

LOCKLEY, R. M. (1954)—*Vet. Record.* 66 : 434

LOCKLEY, R. M. (1961)—*J. Anim. Ecol.* 30 : 385

LOCKLEY, R. M. (1962)—*Nature.* 194 : 988

MARTIN, C. J. (1936)—*Aust. C.S.I.R. Bull.* 96

MCILWAINE, C. P. (1962)—*N.Z. J. Sci.* 5:325

MEAD-BRIGGS, A. R., & A. J. B. RUDGE (1960)—*Nature.* 187:1136

MYERS, K., & W. E. POOLE (1962)—*Aust. J. Ecol.* 10:225

MYKYTOWYCZ, R. (1958-61)—*C.S.I.R.O. Wildl. Res.* 3:7. 4:1. 5:1. 6:142

MYKYTOWYCZ, R. (1962)—*Nature.* 193:799

POOLE, W. E. (1960)—*C.S.I.R.O. Wildl. Res.* 5:21

SOUTHERN, H. N. (1940)—*Ann. Appl. Biol.* 27:509

STEPHENS, M. N. (1952)—*Proc. Zool. Soc. Lond.* 122:417

THACKER, E. J. & C. S. BRANDT (1955)—*J. Nutrition.* 55:375

THOMPSON, H. V., & A. N. WORDEN (1956)—*The Rabbit.* Lond.

WATSON, J. S. (1954)—*Nature.* 184:608

WATSON, J. S. (1957)—*N.Z. J. Sci. Tech.* 38:451

Index of Subjects